CW00976674

Discovering
CHURCHES

John Harries

Shire Publications Ltd.

CONTENTS

Line drawings by Dennis Lack

Copyright © 1972 by John Harries. First published 1972. Reprinted 1976. Second edition 1979, reprinted 1984 and 1988. Number 137 in the 'Discovering' series. ISBN 0 85263 471 4.

Printed in Great Britain by C. I. Thomas & Sons (Haverfordwest) Ltd, Press Buildings, Merlins Bridge, Haverfordwest.

1. INTRODUCTION

There is an incomparable variety in the church architecture of this country, from the gaunt, almost pagan power of Saxon work to the crowded complexity of the Victorians. This architecture takes in the strength of Norman building, the soaring grey stone and light of later medieval churches, the lordly equanimity of Classical ones and, always, the simplicity of the small churches that have evolved by a kind of haphazard genius.

The study of architecture, which in this case is merely the pursuit of more telling observation and comparison, opens our eyes to this variety, and it is upon the architecture of parish churches that this book therefore concentrates, rather than upon their archaeology or associations.

Celtic work (fifth century to twelfth century)

For this reason there is little to be said about early Celtic building. Its style was common to Scotland and Ireland, and had an influence on work in northern England. The best examples are in the south of Ireland. Other remains are fragmentary, and though the earliest churches were made of wood, the only example is in England at Greensted-juxta-Ongar (Essex), and this is Saxon not Celtic. One of the most impressive Celtic buildings in Scotland is the round tower at Brechin (Angus), for example.

There are a few clocháns, or beehive huts, as in the Outer Hebrides, and a few of the single-cell, rectangular oratories that developed from them, especially in Ireland. From the seventh century, mortar was used in the building of these oratories. They epitomize the Celtic style, with their battered walls, antae, massive lintels, and steeply-pitched roofs. This style flourished up to and even beyond the Norman Conquest of 1066, in spite of the Danish raids in the ninth century.

Some of the finest Celtic work went into decorative carving, which involved figures, biblical scenes, and patterns of inter-lace and animals, and was sometimes influenced by Viking work. The outstanding examples of this carving are the high crosses at such places as Ruthwell (Dumfries) and Bewcastle (Cumb).

2. THE PLAN OF THE PARISH CHURCH

The single-cell plan was also adopted for churches in England, but in the seventh century it was given a chancel, which opened from the nave by the chancel arch, and housed the altar. This development did not take place in Ireland and Scotland until the tenth century. The characteristic examples of this early Saxon plan are at Escomb (Durham), Monkwearmouth and Jarrow (Tyne & Wear). These are tall, narrow, impressive churches.

Towards the end of the Saxon period, west towers were sometimes built, often for defence and guidance, when a cresset might be added—an iron basket used to contain a beacon-fire, and supported on a post. The square end to the chancel of these churches testifies to general Celtic influence.

The Roman tradition was also at work, but again examples are rare. The main features of the more ambitious Roman basilican plan were the apse, the aisled nave, the crypt, and the narthex or porch running the width of the church, and covering the three main doors at the west end. The altar had

Norman Interior. A simple interior with an aisle to the south side only. The chancel, originally square, was extended in the Early English period; it has several monumental brasses fixed to the wall. The aisle has a thirteenth-century piscina. Monuments of various periods are on the walls. The pulpit is Victorian, designed to go with the simple Norman lines.

originally been at the western end of the church, as in the fourth century basilica at Silchester (Hants), whose foundations alone remain. But by Saxon times the present arrangement had come into being, and the altar was placed at the eastern end of the church. Aisles were rare in the Saxon period, but basilican-influenced churches were encouraged in the south of England by St. Augustine's mission in 598— though the only proper examples are much later, as at Brixworth (Northants), Wing (Bucks) (tenth century), Repton (Derbys), and Worth (Sussex). This is a cruciform church, and another is St Mary in Castro, Dover (Kent). Saxon and basilican features are often found mixed.

The Normans took naturally to the basilican plan, and based large churches upon it, as at Calne (Wilts) and Melbourne (Derbys). Eventually, the aisled nave passed into the tradition of English church building. Other features were more short-lived, including the apse, the narthex, the crypt, and the elaborate west front. There are fine Norman west fronts at Iffley (Oxon) and Stewkley (Bucks). This feature was superseded by the west tower when that became more common in the thirteenth century.

The Normans also developed the cruciform church, often with a central tower and sometimes with chapels. There are good examples at Portchester (Hants), Old Shoreham (Sussex), and Castor (Cambs). Five round churches, based on the Church of the Holy Sepulchre in Jerusalem, and associated with the Crusaders, were built at Northampton, Cambridge, Little Maplestead (Essex), London, and Ludlow Castle (Salop). St. Nicholas, Orphir (Orkney) is another of these churches.

But the plan of many churches at this time was simply evolved from the one- or two-chambered Saxon plan by adding a west or central tower, and—especially in east and southeast England and in Scotland—by adding an apse. So by the twelfth century a simple parish church might have the plan shown on page 9.

In the thirteenth century, the apse would probably be lengthened into a square-ended chancel, an aisle would be added, and there might also be a transept or transeptal chapel. The fine Norman naves were usually kept. The result would look like the Early English plan on page 9, where the development of this kind of church over the next two centuries is summarized.

Gothic Interior. This shows a church with aisles to the nave using two kinds of Early English columns, but windows of later periods. The chancel is all Early English, with a tie-beam roof and a good fifteenth-century tomb. The pulpit is fifteenth-century, and alongside is the Decorated door to the rood loft and its opening above.

The changes were made necessary by larger congregations, local pride, and the increasing social importance of religion and churches. Aisles and transepts might be given side altars, and 'squints' or small openings through which the main altar could be seen. Porches might also be built on the north of the church, sometimes because the manor-house stood on that side. Additions and improvements were often paid for by ecclesiastics, local benefactors, and later especially by the guilds which met for charitable, religious, and business purposes. A chantry chapel might be endowed by its builder for the saying of masses in his memory.

The general tendency was to greater height, lightness, and elaboration. Clerestories were added, and internal divisions were marked not by walls but by carved screens—parclose screens for chapels, and a rood-screen for the chancel. The rood-screen supported a rood, or crucifix, flanked by the figures of the Virgin and St. John, and it sometimes had a gallery reached by a staircase and used by the choir. Much of the original church would have been replaced; what remained would act as a core.

Not all churches passed through all these stages of development, and many variations were possible. The thirteenth and
fourteenth centuries saw the building of some fine cruciform
churches, such as Uffington (Oxon), and Heckington (Lincs).
Four of these have transeptal aisles—a feature rare even in
cathedrals. They are Melton Mowbray (Leics), Patrington
(Humber), St. Mary Redcliffe (Bristol) (plate 8), and
Faversham (Kent).

New chapels or extended aisles led to a rectangular plan,
and this was common in East Anglia from the fourteenth
century onwards. In Devon and Cornwall a church might
have three naves, each with a gabled roof. Double-naved
fifteenth century churches are found in Clwyd, central
Gwynedd, southern Powys, south-west Dyfed and Cornwall.
St. Helen, Abingdon (Oxon) has four aisles, and Findon
(Sussex) has two naves under one roof.

Great variety was possible in the number, position, and
plan of towers. Melbourne (Derbys) is the only surviving
parish church with three towers, but other churches have two
towers—whether transeptal, both at the west end, or one
western and the other central. A single tower could be at
the end of a transept or aisle, or 'engaged'—that is, partly sunk
between the aisles. Some towers are supported on arches, to
ensure right of way, as at Sandbach (Ches) and St. Mary,
Warwick. Alternatively the tower could be detached, especially
in Herefordshire, Cornwall, and East Anglia. It could be
octagonal, or have an octagonal lantern, often as a prelude to a
spire. Maldon (Essex) has a tower of triangular plan. In East
Anglia and some south-eastern counties, round towers of flint are
common because of a shortage of stone suitable for building
quoins — the stones at the angles of buildings. There are over a
hundred of these towers in Norfolk, and over forty in Suffolk.

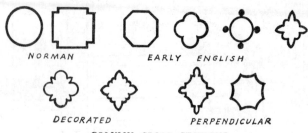

NORMAN   EARLY   ENGLISH

DECORATED   PERPENDICULAR

COLUMN CROSS-SECTIONS

8

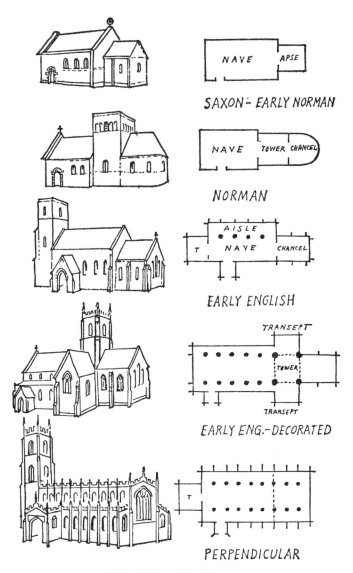

NAVE | APSE

SAXON - EARLY NORMAN

NAVE | TOWER | CHANCEL

NORMAN

AISLE
T | NAVE | CHANCEL

EARLY ENGLISH

TRANSEPT
TOWER
TRANSEPT

EARLY ENG. - DECORATED

T

PERPENDICULAR

MEDIEVAL PLANS

3. THE STRUCTURE OF THE PARISH CHURCH

The Saxon period (600-1066)

By 600 the Saxons had been in England for well over 100 years. But they had not long been Christians—far less long than the Celts, for example. Celtic work has already been mentioned, however, and this section deals with English churches.

The Saxons used the bricks and stones of Roman buildings as often as possible. This was the case at Brixworth (Northants) and Bradwell (Essex), for example. Saxon walls, towers and arches were slender compared to the later Norman ones, though still massive to our eyes: but the emphasis was on height rather than breadth.

Windows were small, and some distance from the ground. They generally had semicircular heads in the Roman tradition, though triangular heads are also characteristic of Saxon work, and both kinds may occur in the same building. Windows were often given a splay, which could be to the inside or outside of the wall, or else to both sides, in which case it is called a double splay. It was quite common, however, for the jambs or sides of windows to be straight—as though the opening had been stamped through the masonry. Windows with two lights, or openings, are often found in towers of the period—the lights being separated by a baluster, or shaped column. At Earls Barton (Northants) (plate 1), there is a tower window with five lights.

The heads of doorways followed similar patterns to those of windows. The jambs sometimes incorporated balusters or carving, but were more often plain. Arches rested upon horizontal stones set in the wall and called imposts, which were either left as rough blocks, or else carved with mouldings.

Saxon masonry is very distinctive. One of its best-known features is long and short work, in which the quoins are alternately upright and horizontal. In the earlier churches, angles were constructed in a more rough-and-ready way. The Saxons were fond of patterned masonry, however, and two other well-known features of their work are pilaster strips and herringboning. Pilaster strips are vertical strips of stone standing out very slightly from the wall, and used purely for decorative purposes. They are sometimes linked, above a string course, by arches of the semicircular or triangular kind. There is pilaster work of varying complexity at Woolbeding and Sompting (Sussex), Repton (Derbys), and Barnack (Cambs)

—among other places. In herringbone work, stones of one course all slope to the right, the stones of the course above it slope to the left, and so on. Saxon masonry was generally covered with plaster—traces of which can still sometimes be seen.

Western towers were common, and nearly seventy survive in England alone. Most of them are in the east coast counties of Northumberland, Durham, Lincolnshire, and East Anglia —and this suggests that they may have been used for defence. These towers are particularly numerous in Lincolnshire, which has 28 of them. Some Saxon churches had no towers, and a few had towers which were not situated in the west. Barton-on-Humber (Humberside) was one of these.

Saxon towers belong to the later part of the period. They often contained a room for the priest, looking on to the nave, and a belfry, with openings to allow the sound of the bells to carry. The tower roofs of this period have since been replaced by parapets or upper storeys, for example, and the only tower with the original type of finish is at Sompting (Sussex) (plate 7). It has a four-sided, gabled roof, forming a blunt spire known as a Rhenish helm, because of its similarity to many examples in the Rhineland. The roofs of Saxon naves are high-pitched. In the last half of the Saxon period, churches were furnished with a piscina—a kind of basin used for rinsing the vessels needed in the mass, and fitted with a drain. The piscina is usually to the south of the altar, and was later set into the wall.

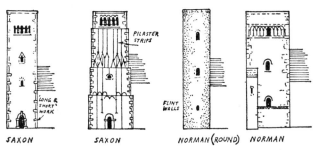

SAXON   SAXON   NORMAN (ROUND)   NORMAN

ROMANESQUE TOWERS

The Norman and Transitional Periods (1066-1200)

A period of energetic church-building followed the Norman Conquest, and it was then that the great British cathedrals started to be built. The Normans built in the style known as Romanesque—and in fact this is the name given to this period in Scotland, where it began and ended later than in England.

In Wales and Scotland, the dominance and austere architectural standards of the Cistercian Order militated against the full growth of Romanesque. The best examples are therefore in England, though there is good work at such places as Dalmeny (W. Lothian), Tywyn (Gwynedd), and Marcross (Glam).

The Normans tended to favour the basilican plan, and the apsidal sanctuary for the housing of the altar. They made the semicircular arch peculiarly their own, and decorated it with bold and varied geometrical patterns. Towers were generally more squat than Saxon ones—and, indeed, the special mark of Norman architecture is its massive quality. This is partly caused by the method of construction, which was to fill stone walls and pillars with a core of rubble, so making them far thicker than the Saxon equivalents. Although this meant that walls sometimes crumbled in later times, such was the quality of work in naves, arcades, towers, doorways, and chancel-arches that these were often kept, and Norman work is reasonably common. Nave arcades often have considerable variety in the piers and arch mouldings. Though some arcades were blind, others were free-standing—and these in particular gave great strength to Norman interiors. This is best seen in larger churches such as Tewkesbury Abbey (Glos), and Romsey Abbey (Hants), but Norman arcades dignify churches wherever they occur.

Norman architecture represented something new and high-powered in British church-building. It started to give it space and weight. The vaulting, and the style of the arcades were particularly important in this respect. Originally, Norman roofs were made of wood, steep in pitch, and boarded in with a flat ceiling. Then came the most basic forms of stone roof—the barrel or tunnel vault, and the groined vault that developed from it. In the later part of the period vaulting was often quadripartite, as at Elkstone (Glos) and Dalmeny (W. Lothian). Vaults were most often reserved for aisles or chancels. In arches, the Saxon impost gave way to the abacus and capital. Block and scalloped capitals were popular, but

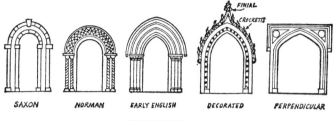

SAXON   NORMAN   EARLY ENGLISH   DECORATED   PERPENDICULAR

DOORWAYS

capitals were sometimes more elaborately carved with animals, religious scenes, stylized foliage, or pure pattern.

At first, piers were rectangular, though often compound—that is, with shafts or slender columns added to their faces, or let into their angles. Many Norman piers, however, are simply cylindrical—a fact that accounts for the power of the nave arcade at Melbourne (Derbys), for example. Columns were also given low bases and plinths. Shafts were carried on by the orders of arches, which took on the appearance of recessed rings of stone diminishing in size. Originally, arches were square-cut, again as though they had been stamped straight through the wall. But eventually their mouldings were ornamented with chevrons, billets, lozenge-work, or beakheads. In later Norman work, these patterns were continued on the shafts of columns, and the capital and abacus were often abandoned, so that the moulding could go right round an opening—as in the beautiful east window at Elkstone (Glos).

One of the chief glories of Norman churches is the detail which sets off the broad simplicity of surface and design. This detail makes many Norman doorways into works of art which radiate exuberance. There are excellent examples at Fingest (Bucks), Portchester Priory (Hants), Barfreston (Kent), Steetley Chapel (Derbys), and Ewenny Priory (Glam). The unusual doorway at Kilpeck (Herefs) is decorated with grotesques, as well as foliage and other patterns. Grotesque creatures also figure in the tympana of Ridlington and Egleton (Leics). Tympana are common in Norman doorways, and some other good examples are to be found at Siddington, Elkstone, Quenington, Sherborne, and North Cerney (Glos), and at South Weald (Essex). They depict such things as the Lives of the Saints and the Harrowing of Hell. In later Norman times, the chancel-arch was also decorated. Apart from this, the opening sometimes had an arch on each side, and these

13

additional arches could be either open or blind.

In the grander churches clerestories were added, generally above a triforium. Most Norman windows were small, set high in the walls, and deeply splayed. It was at this time that windows started to be given mullions—uprights dividing a window into two or more lights. This represented a clear advance on the Saxon use of a dividing baluster. In larger churches, one may sometimes find circular windows, and from this type developed wheel windows, with shafts radiating from the centre. These windows are akin to continental rose-windows, and are rare in this country. In the later part of the Norman period, the piscina was often set in the wall next to sedilia, though sometimes it stood on its own pillar.

The most distinctive contribution the Normans made to exterior decoration was arcading. Windows and doorways were placed between a pair of blind arches, so that an ornamental arcade was formed. This arrangement is often found in the belfry of a tower, and sometimes open arches are alternated with blind ones. Eventually, one finds whole arcades of blind arches, with or without an occasional opening, and the final version of this embellishment is the interlacing arcade. Alternatives were a blind trellis pattern and a pattern made of scales. Buttresses were needed to help support the weight of stone vaulting—though as walls were very thick, buttresses did not need to be as substantial as they were later to become. They are usually flat, plain, and of only one stage.

Many tower roofs have been replaced by parapets, pinnacles, spires, or steeples, but the type of roof most often used was a low, pyramidal structure. There must also have been taller spires, however, including some of octagonal form emerging from a square base, as at East Meon (Hants). Other towers were covered by gabled roofs called saddlebacks, and these are reasonably common, especially in South Wales, Gloucestershire, Cornwall, Northamptonshire, and Oxfordshire. Fingest (Bucks) has a reconstructed roof with double gables, while Llansannor (Glam) has a four-gabled roof.

Not all west towers were square: some had an oblong plan, and round towers were still common in East Anglia. The plan of Norman towers was sometimes varied by the addition of a turret staircase, whether rectangular or circular. Corbel tables were introduced beneath the eaves to help support the roof, and could be carved with faces, as at Kilpeck (Herefs). Niches were occasionally placed over doorways or arches to house carved religious figures.

In the last half of the twelfth century, a gradual change came over Norman architecture. The most important feature of this evolution was the pointed arch, which was associated with the development of the rib vault. In addition, windows tended to be larger and more deeply splayed, and columns had more elaborate bases and sections. The capitals, too, were more precisely cut, with the form known as stiff-leaf foliage. Mouldings were undercut and sometimes chamfered or bevelled. All these features were to usher in the Early English period, and mark the beginning of Gothic as opposed to Norman.

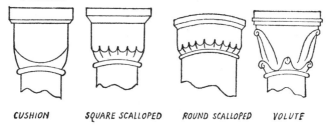

CUSHION   SQUARE SCALLOPED   ROUND SCALLOPED   VOLUTE

NORMAN CAPITALS

The new features were combined with Norman or Romanesque ones for a while, so this is known as the Transitional period. A pointed chancel-arch might be enriched with Norman mouldings, for example, or a nave-arcade given Norman arches and Early English piers. The various combinations are numerous, and good examples can be seen at Burpham, Pagham, and New Shoreham (Sussex), Waddesdon (Bucks), St. John, and St. Peter, Winchester (Hants), Rothbrook (Northants), the Temple Church (London), Llanaber (Gwynedd), Llanbadarn Fawr (Dyfed), and Moulton (Lincs).

Early English Gothic (1200-1300)

This period tends to be known as Early Pointed in Scotland. During it, walls became thinner, though still often built in the Norman way, windows were enlarged, and buttresses were given greater projection, so as to take the weight of the stone vaulting. All this gave a lighter effect to churches—an effect which was heightened by the pointed arch and slender columns, and set off by increasingly delicate carving. This style had the clarity and vigour of discovery.

Windows were soon elongated into the slender, pointed lancets that are one of the chief marks of Early English style.

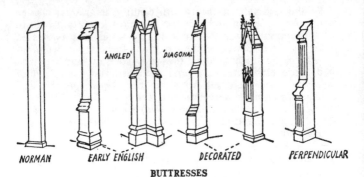

BUTTRESSES

Lancet windows set in side-walls are usually single, but at the east or west end they are often combined—in the doublet, for example, though this is rare. The wall above a doublet could be pierced with an additional opening. Such openings, whether circular, trefoil, or quatrefoil gave rise to plate tracery—the precursor of the more elaborate traceries of intersecting ribwork that developed in the later middle ages. Windows were still splayed inside. Lancets were often arranged in triplets, with the central light raised above the other two, so that the whole window suggested the pointed shape. This was the most popular pattern for the east end of a church, especially in Sussex, though there are many cases elsewhere. Bosham (Sussex) has a window of five lancets, and Ockham (Surrey) has a seven-light window.

The pointed arch was also used for doorways, and the tympanum fell into disfavour, though one or two fine instances remain, as at Higham Ferrers (Northants). The chancel was often vaulted in stone at this time, in the groined and ribbed manner, and sometimes transverse and longitudinal ribs were added to the diagonal ones. Stoke d'Abernon (Surrey), Berkhamsted (Herts), and Hythe (Kent) all contain excellent vaulting.

The square Norman abacus gave way to the round form made up of roll-mouldings, and capitals became more ornate. They were decorated with stylized foliage, as in the beautiful examples at West Walton (Norf), Stone (Kent), and St. Mary, Shrewsbury (Salop). Bell capitals, which look as though they have been turned on a lathe, are also fairly common. Under-cutting continued in mouldings and columns—so much so that shafts are sometimes detached. Mouldings were often decorated with dog-tooth ornament, which consists of small, pyramidal shapes linked in a row.

Towers were decorated with pointed arcading, but the two most distinctive features of exteriors were the increased size of windows, especially in the belfry-stage of the tower, and the development of more ambitious and better-proportioned spires. Spires were generally made of wood or stone, and early examples were square in section, though later on the octagonal shape predominated. Fitting this to a square tower presented a problem, since there was a triangle left at each corner of the base. These triangles could be masked with parapets, or with pinnacles, but a more common method was to cover them with small, semi-pyramidal roofs. This produced the broach spire, which is typical of the thirteenth century, though later examples are found.

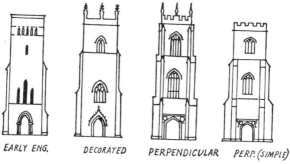

EARLY ENG.   DECORATED   PERPENDICULAR   PERP. (SIMPLE)

GOTHIC TOWERS

Alternatively, the square base could be joined by sloping roofs to the octagon, whose diagonal sides would then be brought to a point at the angles of the tower. This kind of spire was often shingled, or 'tiled' in lead or wood. The eaves rested on corbel-tables. Later in the century, particularly in east Leicestershire and Northamptonshire, broach spires were adorned with spirelights, or graduated tiers of gabled dormer windows. Sometimes tower and spire are replaced by a western bell-gable surmounted by a cross. Porches often had gabled roofs.

Early English work is fairly widespread, and Kent, Lincolnshire, Surrey and Sussex are particularly rich in this respect. The following churches are complete or outstanding examples: Eaton Bray (Beds), Uffington (Oxon), Ottery St. Mary (Devon), Darlington (Durham), Hythe and Westwell (Kent),

West Walton (Norf), Strixton (Northants), Hexham (Northumb), Climping (Sussex), Potterne (Wilts), and Skelton (Yorks).

The bases of columns often consisted of a roll moulding, and were occasionally encircled by a seat. Clerestories were still rare. Doorways contained several orders, and were sometimes double. Both doors and windows often had a hood-mould or dripstone above them—a moulding which sheltered the window itself. The ends rested upon corbels, which were sometimes carved, with faces for example—as were the gargoyles, or spouts used to drain water from behind parapets. String courses divided the church into its different stages.

Sedilia were elaborated, as at Rushden (Northants) and Uffington (Oxon). Double piscinas were introduced, one basin being used by the priest for washing his hands, and the other for washing the holy vessels. Figure-niches also increased in variety and number. Buttresses were topped by a slope, a gable, or a pinnacle.

A simple type of church which persisted until the nineteenth century was developed in Scotland at this time. But on the whole the parish church was neglected there in favour of abbeys and cathedrals, and anyhow most Early Pointed work has been altered. Good examples survive, however, at Kilchrist (Ross), Mortlach (Banffs), Dunstaffnage Chapel, and St. Brendan's Chapel near Skipness Castle (Argyll). North walls were generally built without windows in Scotland, in order to make churches less bleak.

As well as many humble churches, and some slightly more elaborate ones such as Beddgelert (Dyfed), Wales has full-scale work of the period at Grosmont (Gwent), St. Mary, Brecon (Powys), Cheriton and Llantwit Major (Glam), and St. Mary, Haverfordwest (Dyfed).

The general effect of the innovations of this time has often been exaggerated. Many Early English interiors, especially in smaller churches, show only a halting transition from Norman to Gothic, with simple lancets, and uncertainty about proportions—particularly those of arches and piers. These churches are often very beguiling, but they contain, in the odd pointed arch or lancet, the merest promise that architecture is going to become more sophisticated.

It is in the larger churches that this promise begins to be realized, though even they are not always as free of Norman weight as is often made out, and in many cases there is still some confusion over proportions. In a very few cases one can say that something quite new has been achieved, as at Pershore

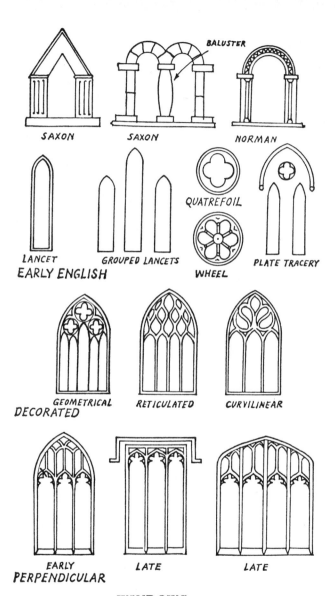

BALUSTER

SAXON   SAXON   NORMAN

LANCET   GROUPED LANCETS   QUATREFOIL   WHEEL   PLATE TRACERY

EARLY ENGLISH

GEOMETRICAL   RETICULATED   CURVILINEAR

DECORATED

EARLY
PERPENDICULAR   LATE   LATE

WINDOWS

19

Abbey (Worcs) and Abbey Dore (Herefs). In these churches there is a feeling of liberation from the heavily encrusted and bowed weight of Norman churches, splendid as their power and volume could sometimes be. Norman mouldings are rich and varied, but essentially based on repetition: they are accretions of decorative wealth. These few Early English examples take this hoarded vitality and release it in simpler and more sweeping lines, and with this a new spirit enters church architecture.

Decorated Gothic (1300-1350)

This rather ascetic spirit soon relaxed into the luxuriance of the Decorated period. Detail proliferated, and line became more sinuous, especially in the characteristic form of curve known as ogee—though many churches remained relatively simple. Decorated work continued the tendency towards lighter and more open construction. Not only were churches often extended and enlarged, but stone was pared away wherever possible. The stone infilling of window-arches was cut away until only slender tracery was left, and arches were increased in area. The flying buttress was devised as a way of carrying the thrust of the roof and of clerestory walls across the widened aisles in a graceful and economical arc.

The development of the window is one of the main features of the Decorated period. Plate tracery eventually arrived at a geometrical phase, in which the head of the window was filled with circles or foiled circles having only slender ribwork between them. This continued until a late stage, and is sometimes found combined with bar tracery, in which the pattern springs directly from the lines of the mullions. A basic form of this is intersected tracery, where the 'branches' of mullions cut across each other to make a simple mesh. Later, the branches became more undulating, and formed curvilinear or flowing tracery, and reticulated tracery. Reticulated tracery consists of a network of circles drawn at top and bottom into ogee shapes. By this stage the ribwork was often cusped— that is, elaborated by small pointed projections of the sort occurring between the lobes of a trefoil. Sometimes Decorated windows have flat heads, and circular windows of wheel or foliated form are more common in this period.

The ogee curve is found in the sections of mouldings, and in arches of all kinds, as in the sedilia and Easter sepulchre at Hawton (Notts). Here, the canopies are carved with such profuse foliage that they seem to be weighed down by a mass of vegetation; the carving is skilful, but the effect is almost too florid. Easter sepulchres are canopied recesses set in the chancel wall and used to contain the sacrament or effigy of Christ at Easter. There are other examples at Patrington (**Humber**), and Heckington and Navenby (Lincs).

Another decorative feature, as typical of the fourteenth century as the dog-tooth was of the thirteenth, is the ballflower. It was repeated on the roll-mouldings of windows and arches, on mullions, and on spires and pinnacles. These were also decorated with crockets and finials—small, leaf-shaped projections. The first belong to the slope of a pinnacle, for example, the second to its top. Crockets are also found clustered on hoodmoulds of all kinds, and on niches.

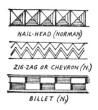
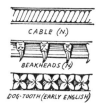

NAIL-HEAD (NORMAN)   CABLE (N.)   BALLFLOWER (DECORATED)

ZIG-ZAG OR CHEVRON (N.)   BEAKHEADS (N.)   RUNNING VINE (DEC. AND PERP.)

BILLET (N.)   DOG-TOOTH (EARLY ENGLISH)   SQUARE FLOWER (PERP.)

CARVED MOULDINGS

Amid all this elaboration, pillars were often less complicated than their thirteenth century counterparts. They sometimes had an octagonal section, which is very distinguished, or four shafts attached to a central column. Plain capitals were common, but lavish churches such as Patrington (Humber) contain capitals carved with foliage that is both more involved and slightly more naturalistic than in the previous period.

All the forms of ornament mentioned are found in dense concentration in the canopied arcading of sedilia, piscinas, and tombs. Piscinas are often simple, though one occasionally finds combinations such as a double piscina with triple sedilia. Stone vaulting became more elaborate, since decorative ribs such as liernes were added to the structural ones to make star-shaped designs. The intersections were covered by bosses—small projections often carved with foliage, just as corbels were. Fine vaulting, which is a feature of this period, is usually found in the chancel or porch, as at St. Mary Redcliffe (Bristol). The triforium, if there were one, would be smaller, so that larger arcades and clerestories could be accommodated.

As far as the exterior goes, buttresses now projected more, and often consisted of several stages. While the plain kind of buttress with a sloping top was still common, others were

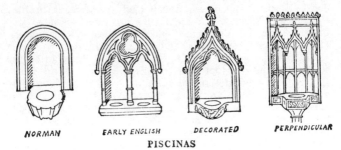

NORMAN   EARLY ENGLISH   DECORATED   PERPENDICULAR

PISCINAS

decorated with niches and pinnacles. The broach spire was generally superseded by taller and more graceful constructions, with parapets and four or more pinnacles at the base. These pinnacles were sometimes topped off by flying buttresses. Octagonal lanterns began to appear as a transitional stage between tower and spire, as at Patrington (Humber) and Wilby (Northants). Spirelights and crockets both add to the detail of Decorated spires.

Stair-turrets and the buttresses placed at the angles of towers were tapered so as to enhance the silhouettes of churches and spires. Belfry openings often filled the upper storey of the tower, and were sometimes combined in pairs. Round ventilation holes were let into the ringing-chambers of towers. Central towers were sometimes octagonal in form, and Uffington (Oxon) shows that this can be a satisfying arrangement.

Scotland was at war with England for most of the fourteenth century, and this meant that few churches were built there. Fife was relatively quiet, however, and has several fine churches of the period, the main example being St. Monan's, Firth of Forth. The Decorated style persisted into the fifteenth century in Scotland, as is shown by Roslin (Midlothian) and the ruined Lincluden (Kirkcudbright)—both Collegiate churches.

There is rather more building of this period in Wales, though political isolation from England, and the sway of the Cistercians meant that Decorated work was not as prominent as in England. The best examples include Caerwys (Clwyd), Llanidloes (Powys), and Coity and Coychurch (Glam).

NORMAN   EARLY ENGLISH   DECORATED   PERPENDICULAR

SEDILIA

Perpendicular Gothic (1350-1660)

The Black Death occurred in the middle of the century, and the continuous line of architectural development was broken. A new style was already evolving in London, however—though it first fully emerged at Gloucester Cathedral, where work was carried on during the Black Death. It was to be the unchallenged style in church building for nearly the next 300 years, so it is the most widely found of all in British churches—and in fact it is a uniquely British style of architecture. It is called Perpendicular, because the bowed lines of Decorated windows and arches gave way to uprights that only curved briefly at the top, forming a much flatter kind of head. The general proportions are in keeping with this: arcades, naves, columns, and towers are lofty and graceful.

Churches were becoming more rectangular in plan, and this simplified their interior appearance. The impression is often of a spacious hall with a vista of arcading and clerestory leading to great east and west windows. The interior seems to be covered with a light mesh of surface decoration. For the most part this is rectilinear, as in the cusped panels of walls, the coffering of ceilings, and the mullions and transoms of windows. But this framework is set off by the beautiful curves of arcade mouldings and vaulting ribs. The filigree of screen-work enriches the view without interrupting it. The walls seem more glass than stone, and the decoration weaves a web to catch the light.

For all the delicacy of their ornament, these churches were planned along simpler lines than Decorated ones. This had an immediate practical advantage, since there was a shortage of skilled labour after the Black Death. But it also had aesthetic advantages, since it is this simplicity that gives these churches their coherence and splendour. The soaring uprights fuse exaltation and austerity in one of the most haunting paradoxes in architecture.

Perpendicular was developed quickly, and though it was often combined with Decorated features for a while, especially in East Anglia, by the end of the century it was the dominant style. With the growth of the merchant class, churches received a new influx of funds. The wool trade in particular prospered, and this accounts for the series of 'wool' churches in East Anglia and the West Country. There are first-class examples at St. Mary Redcliffe (Bristol) (plate 8), Northleach and Chipping Campden (Glos), Newbury (Berks), Yeovil (Som), Cricklade (Wilts), Lavenham, Blythburgh, and Long Melford (Suff), Dedham (Essex), Great Ponton (Lincs), and Sall (Norf).

The features of the style are these. Cusped panelling occurs on buttresses, columns, fonts, pulpits, tombs, and doors—as well as on the walls of naves and towers. Windows are larger, and though ribwork was still occasionally in a Decorated style, on the whole tracery is rectilinear: it is also often more inventive than is supposed. Sometimes windows occupy a whole wall, as at St. Nicholas, King's Lynn (Norf), where the west window has eleven lights. This increased size made an ideal setting for stained glass. Clerestories were added or enlarged, except in Cornwall and Devon, where they were not popular—and triforia became more perfunctory.

Window-arches are usually either pointed or four-centred, though the heads of windows could also be flat, segmental, or ogee. As the period wore on, the four-centred arch became increasingly common, in arcading as well as in windows and doors, until it foreshadowed the Tudor arch. In doorways the four-centred arch is often enclosed in a square label or hood-mould. Spandrels, the triangular spaces between the arch and the label, are often decorated with cusped panels or circles, or else with heraldic devices.

Columns became more slender, and were still often octagonal, with or without concave sides, or cusped panelling—though that is rare. The section of compound piers was often lozenge-shaped. In some churches, arch-mouldings ran on into the shafts, which then had unobtrusive capitals, or in a few cases none at all. Elsewhere, capitals ran right round the pier, or were decorated with carved foliage or figures. Vaulting sprang from the arcade pillars, and not from corbels as before. Pier bases were generally taller than they had been in the Decorated period.

Subsidiary detail was everywhere. Endless invention was shown in carving corbels, gargoyles, hood-moulds, and bosses. They could include emblems such as shields, beasts, and the

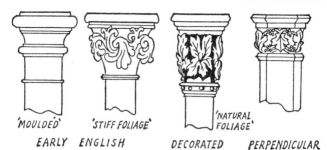

'MOULDED'   'STIFF FOLIAGE'   'NATURAL FOLIAGE'

EARLY ENGLISH   DECORATED   PERPENDICULAR

GOTHIC CAPITALS

Tudor rose and portcullis, or else the crossed keys of St. Peter, and the Five Wounds of Christ. They could be carved with portraits, with figures symbolizing the Seven Deadly Sins and the Seven Virtues, or—in the case of corbels and gargoyles—with grotesques and demons. The habit of carving corbels and gargoyles in this way had developed in the fourteenth century, and by the fifteenth century had become an enjoyable art, full of humour and individuality.

The four-leaved flower was used as much as the dog-tooth and the ballflower had been in previous periods. Sedilia and piscinas were often intricately carved. Figure niches were common, and were often covered by miniature canopies, battlements, or pinnacles. Such tabernacle-work is repeated in stained glass, fonts, pulpits, sedilia and piscinas, screens, tombs, and in the stalls or rows of carved seats in the choir or chancel. The reredos, or devotional screen covering the wall behind the altar, came into prominence. Often it is of stone, alabaster, or wood, and sometimes it consists of carved figures, as at Ludlow (Salop).

Many of the architectural forms mentioned were used to adorn the church furniture of the period—and there were more kinds of furniture, including stalls, pews, font-canopies, and extra screens. Some screens were made of stone, but by this time woodwork had become one of the glories of parish churches, especially in East Anglia and the West Country.

The beautiful form of vaulting, characteristic of British work and known as fan vaulting, was also developed. The most famous examples are in cathedrals and in the great abbeys and chapels, but it also occurs at Ottery St. Mary and Cullompton (Devon), St. Mary's, Warwick, Spalding (Lincs), and Maids Moreton (Bucks), for example. Not all vaulting was

25

so complicated, but as in the last period, some churches were given lierne vaults. There are very good examples at Cricklade (Wilts), Southwold (Suff), and Northleach (Glos). Both fan and lierne vaults are most commonly found in porches, towers and chapels.

Chapels were built in considerable numbers. Some such as the beautiful Beauchamp Chapel of St Mary's, Warwick have great splendour, and many are dedicated to the Virgin Mary, who was held in special affection. Long Melford (Suff) (plate 11) has an exceptionally fine Lady Chapel at its east end, beyond the altar and vestry, and almost separate from the main building. There might be several altars in a church, founded by various guilds, and chantry chapels were sometimes added, as at Burford (Oxon) and Lavenham (Suff).

Towers and porches are both major features of the period. As well as offering shelter, porches were used in weddings, baptisms, and penances—and for trading, legal business, and fairs.

Porches were sometimes furnished with stone seats, and often contained niches for the figures of saints, and stoups or small stone basins which were filled with holy water. The upper storeys of porches were used for parish or guild meetings; as chapels, court-rooms, and treasuries; and as chambers for nightwatchmen, priests, or families during services—in which case the room might be fitted with a fireplace, and a window overlooking the nave. Later, porches served as reliquaries, armour-stores or general storerooms, and as libraries, parish archives, or schoolrooms. The porches of Bruton (Som), Burford (Oxon), and Cirencester (Glos) all have three storeys.

Perpendicular towers are often works of art in their own right, and a selection is indicated in the gazetteer. Norfolk and Suffolk are especially rich in them, and the local variety is simple and dignified. West doors are common, and so is flushwork—a pattern of stone strips inlaid with flint. Towers generally have battlements, and sometimes each merlon, or raised part of the battlement, is in the form of steps. Pinnacles are modest, or replaced by small figures.

Somerset towers are also famous. The proportions are stately, and since the local stone is specially suitable for carving, the detail is rich and impressive. It includes pierced parapets and belfry-louvres, crests of pinnacles, and niched and canopied saints.

Gloucestershire has some fine towers, which often recall those of Somerset, though parapets and pinnacles are generally

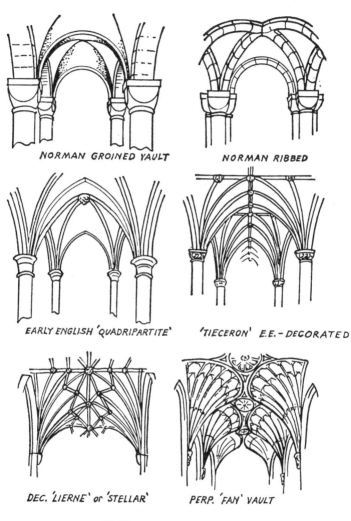

NORMAN GROINED VAULT

NORMAN RIBBED

EARLY ENGLISH 'QUADRIPARTITE'

'TIECERON' E.E. - DECORATED

DEC. 'LIERNE' or 'STELLAR'

PERP. 'FAN' VAULT

VAULTED CEILINGS

simpler. Panelling is a feature of some towers.

Devonshire towers are made of sandstone, not limestone, and this means that they are simpler and more rugged than Somerset towers, and form a pleasant contrast to them. The characteristic use of stair-turrets adds to their bluff appearance. Much the same remarks apply to Cornish towers, which are built of granite.

Other counties have produced fine work, but not as consistently as those already mentioned. They include Wiltshire, Dorset, Cambridgeshire, Northamptonshire, Lincolnshire, Cheshire, Lancashire, Yorkshire, Kent, the border counties of North Wales, and the coastal ones of South Wales.

Several towers of the period have octagonal upper storeys —among them being those at Colyton (Devon), Fotheringay (Northants), and Boston (Lincs). 'Boston Stump' as it is sometimes called is 288 feet tall, and is the tallest church tower in Britain. Battlemented stair-turrets were sometimes added to the eastward part of the church, as at Clare (Suff).

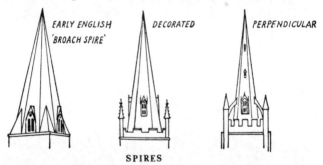

EARLY ENGLISH 'BROACH SPIRE'   DECORATED   PERPENDICULAR

SPIRES

Some of the finest spires in the country date from this period, and there are excellent examples at Louth, Uffington, and Moulton (Lincs), Kettering, King's Sutton and Oundle (Northants), Halsall (Lancs), Yaxley (Cambs), Rotherham (Yorks), Whittlesey (Cambs), Bloxham (Oxon), and Thaxted (Essex). The grace of such spires is often increased by flying buttresses springing from the pinnacles. In Scotland, a hollow pinnacled crown was sometimes used instead of the normal kind of spire, as at St. Giles, Edinburgh, and the Tron Church in Glasgow. St. Nicholas, Newcastle upon Tyne has the same type of crown. There are one or two other local varieties of spire. Broach spires, for example, are largely confined to Leicestershire and Northamptonshire in this period, and

28

slender lead spires are typical of Hertfordshire.

Wales was now reconciled with England and although small churches with bell-cotes were still being built, the Perpendicular style established itself as one of the high points of Welsh architecture, in a form very similar to its English one. There are fine examples at Gresford and Wrexham (Clwyd) (plate 9), St. John, Cardiff (Glam), Old Radnor (Powys), and Tenby (Dyfed).

Scotland had managed to shake off English rule, and so a national Gothic style was developed at last. As prosperity increased, several large town churches were built, including St. John, Perth, the Holy Rood, Stirling, and St. Michael, Linlithgow (W. Lothian). Many rich collegiate churches were built, so that masses could be said for the founder and his family by a college of secular canons. In this, they replaced the monasteries, which were gradually losing support. Typical Scottish features at this time were: double west doorways under round-headed arches; steeply pitched roofs of stone slabs with a broken ridge line; three-sided apses, and—also showing French influence—flamboyant or wavy tracery; crow-stepped or 'corbie' gables; and the crown finish to towers. The Scottish style of this period is rugged, massive, and individual.

The Reformation

In the first half of the sixteenth century British ecclesiastical building suffered a number of setbacks. There was an abundant number of churches already, so not many new buildings were needed; Henry VIII, head of the English Church from 1535, dissolved the monasteries, chantries, and guilds; and many churches were plundered out of greed or the desire to destroy idolatry. Attempts were made to stop this damage in the reigns of Mary and Elizabeth, but it persisted, and in addition a new austerity was brought to parish churches by the Reformation—the movement culminating in 1559 in England whereby greater independence was to be gained from the Roman Church, and its doctrines and practices revised.

'Images, shrines, tabernacles, rood loftes and monuments of idolatrie' were removed, wall paintings were covered with whitewash, and churches were fitted with pulpits—which became the main feature of the interior. The Holy Communion table was substituted for the altar, and roods and their lofts were replaced by the royal arms, and the texts of the Lord's Prayer and Ten Commandments. What stained glass had not been destroyed or replaced with plain glass was allowed to remain, however—but this was largely because of the expense of reglazing.

As a result of these circumstances, fewer churches were built in the second half of the century than at almost any other time, and those that were built are in the old style, apart from some Tudor features such as square-headed windows. The chief examples of the period are Watton (Humber), Woodham Walter (Essex), the rebuilding of Framlingham (Suff)—all dating from about the mid century—and Easton Royal (Wilts), from 1591.

In Scotland, much damage was done by English armies and, at the Reformation, by John Knox's Calvinism. For fifty years afterwards, very few churches were built, though many were adapted. Some of the older churches were abandoned in whole or in part, since only what was needed for preaching purposes was retained. Others were given a transeptal aisle, usually on the north side, and often containing a 'loft' and burial vault. This gave rise to the Scottish T-plan which became established in the seventeenth century, and remained a typical pattern until the nineteenth century. The first important church to be built after the Reformation, however, was the square one at Burntisland (Fife).

By the end of the sixteenth century, the Renaissance or 'rebirth' of architecture inspired by the Classical buildings of ancient Rome had run its course in Italy. But in this country Perpendicular Gothic continued to be the main style for parish churches until the 1650s—though Classicism had already asserted itself in domestic architecture by then.

In the first half of the seventeenth century, the restrictions on church building already mentioned still prevailed, and in addition there were the Civil War and Commonwealth to contend with. So although there was a certain amount of rebuilding, not many churches were built, and a considerable number were destroyed by the Puritans. Among the new churches were Groombridge (Kent), Leighton Bromswold (Hunts), and a few examples associated with the 'Laudian Revival' that followed the appointment of William Laud as Bishop of London in 1628. These include St. John's, Leeds (Yorks), St. Katherine Cree (London) and, dating from the Commonwealth, Staunton Harold (Leics).

Laud adapted many churches as, for the opposite reasons, the Puritans were later to do. Laud wished to stress the holiness of religion, placed the altar at the east end, and surrounded it with altar rails in the Elizabethan manner. The

Puritans emphasized the common sense of worship, brought the table forward, and often destroyed the rails—though it was not long before they were replaced.

But none of these buildings or alterations seriously challenged the sway of Gothic—and nor did the use of Classical forms in monuments and fittings in the sixteenth century, and in such features as nave-arcades as well in the seventeenth century. The very act of building a church in these times was a conservative one.

There were two clear exceptions to the ascendency of Gothic: Inigo Jones's church of St. Paul's, Covent Garden (London) in 1631—the first Classical parish church in the country—and the porch added to St. Mary's, Oxford in 1637, and designed by Nicholas Stone.

Like the rest of Inigo Jones's splendid and innovatory work, St. Paul's owes a debt to Andrea Palladio (1518-80), in its regard for antiquity, its formality, and its strength. Few things could be less like it than the flamboyant porch of St. Mary's. Yet both point to a revolution in taste that eventually produced some of our most successful churches, and both therefore mark the beginning of the end of Gothic. But they were portents, isolated in their single-minded Classicism, and they did not finish Gothic off. Although Classical churches such as Berwick (Northumb) were built from this time on, for the next thirty to forty years they were still so few and so heavily modified by Gothic feeling that they cannot be said to oust Gothic, let alone to follow the rigorous example of Inigo Jones.

Seventeenth century Classicism

Classicism was finally and triumphantly established in this country after the Restoration of 1660 by the work of Sir Christopher Wren (1632-1723). Wren developed an English version of Baroque—the style that, on the Continent, had already dissolved and divided the stability represented by Palladio, and thrown it into a state of ferment. The vocabulary of Classical tradition was extended to include such things as broken pediments and twisted or rusticated columns, and these elements were articulated in a new rhetoric, dwelling on decorative conceits, and swerving and soaring after its own wayward instinct.

English Baroque never sought the dazzling extravagance of continental work, and instead it evolved as an idiom of ample power and more stately rhythms. But it still improvises and concentrates form in a way that contrasts strongly with the clean-cut decorum ordained by tradition for Inigo Jones.

Wren made Baroque into one of the great English styles. His work undoubtedly has its faults, but it is often astonishingly elegant and lively in its detail, and majestic in the way it wields mass and space. It is in such a small church as St. Stephen Walbrook (London)—one of the many churches Wren adapted to cramped sites by using plans as varied as a figure with ten sides, and the Greek cross, with its four equal arms. The best of Wren's steeples are faultless, and together they are the product of a striking vision.

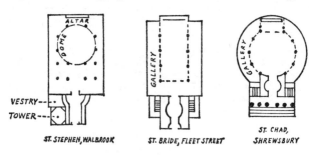

ST. STEPHEN, WALBROOK   ST. BRIDE, FLEET STREET   ST. CHAD, SHREWSBURY

CLASSICAL PLANS

It was Wren who conceived the idea of adding steeples to Classical churches, and who developed the auditory plan that became the pattern for town churches throughout the Classical period. His churches were spacious galleried halls where everyone could see and hear the service. Wren also introduced the central dome to British churches—and he designed 52 churches for the City of London in about forty years, to replace those destroyed in the Great Fire of 1666. But, above all, it is movement that we feel in Wren's work, the vital force of intelligence: shape follows shape as thought from thought, in a fugue of invention drawn at last to a sonorous close. It was this that enabled Wren to shape the City of London, and the architecture of an age.

Some of the elements distinguishing that architecture are as follows. There were five different orders of pillars: Doric, Ionic, and Corinthian from ancient Greece; Tuscan and Composite from ancient Rome. Entrances were in the form of porticos, and arches were semicircular with large keystones—as in the windows, which were large and filled with clear

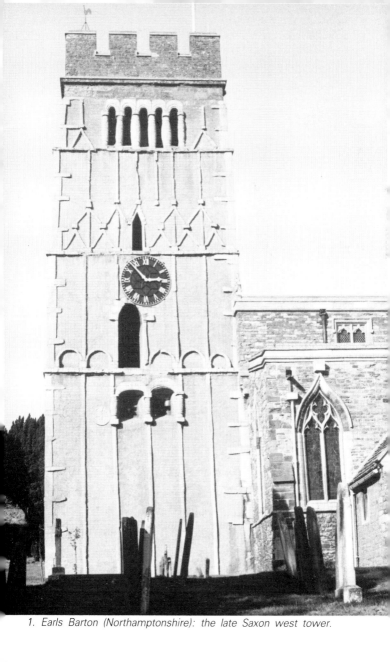

1. Earls Barton (Northamptonshire): the late Saxon west tower.

2. *Great Tey (Essex): a fine example of a Norman tower.*
3. *Greensted-juxta-Ongar (Essex): St Andrew's is the only wooden Saxon church to have survived. The nave is built of split oak but the chancel is a more recent addition.*

4. Lavenham (Suffolk): one of the finest of the East Anglian 'wool churches', in the Perpendicular style.

5. Fairford (Gloucestershire): St Mary's is a Cotswold 'wool church' built in the late fifteenth century.

6. Grantham (Lincolnshire): the magnificent spire of St Wulfram's church, added in the fourteenth century, rises to 272 feet (83 m).

7. Sompting (West Sussex): the unique 'Rhenish helm' tower dates from the eleventh century.

8. St Mary Redcliffe, Bristol (Avon): one of the few English churches with transeptal aisles.

9. Wrexham (Clwyd): an outstanding example of a Perpendicular tower.

10. *Evercreech (Somerset): the fine Perpendicular tower.*

glass. Round windows, too, were common. Ashlar masonry was used for walls, and angles were often emphasized by rustication. Brick was also a fairly standard building material.

A wide variety of Classical mouldings was employed, and various patterns were devised for the gilded and painted plaster ceilings—often with great elegance. Windows and woodwork were decorated with swags of leaves, flowers and fruit, and woodwork in particular was laden with carvings of cherubs and foliage. Pulpit, reredos, font, and organ case all received this treatment, and the master of the craft was Grinling Gibbons. Wren himself did not always design the fittings for his churches, but they enhance his architecture and are often very impressive.

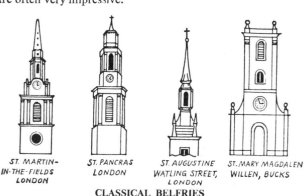

ST. MARTIN-IN-THE-FIELDS LONDON   ST. PANCRAS LONDON   ST. AUGUSTINE WATLING STREET, LONDON   ST. MARY MAGDALEN WILLEN, BUCKS

CLASSICAL BELFRIES

Apart from a few churches such as the Tron Church, Edinburgh, begun in 1637 by the King's Master Mason, John Mylne, there is no evidence of any very decided Classical feeling in Scotland until the last quarter of the century. By that stage, architects such as Sir William Bruce had helped to introduce the Renaissance to Scotland. Then we get churches such as the roofless Tulliallan (Fife), and eventually Canongate, Edinburgh, and Durisdeer (Dumfries). But Tulliallan still contains a large admixture of Gothic—as the Tron Church does—and this was the way for most of the century, though Gothic was gradually being simplified towards Classicism.

It was carried on, however, by large churches such as Greyfriars, Edinburgh, now rebuilt, by more modest ones such as Dairsie (Fife) and Careston (Angus), and by the steeple of Fife, for example. Notable seventeenth century churches included Ayr—built during the Commonwealth—and Largs (Ayrs). Throughout the seventeenth century, very simple traditional churches were still being built in country districts, though in Aberdeenshire there was a fashion for elaborate belfries.

A few churches in Wales contain Classical features, but by the second half of the century a start had been made on building Nonconformist chapels. These did use elements of Classical design, but their spirit was opposed to its studied development, and the general style is a simple domestic one that often has great charm—as at Maes-yr-Onen, Glasbury (Powys) and Llanfihangel a'r arth (Dyfed). The same applies to the chapels that were being built elsewhere, as at Winslow (Bucks), and Walpole (Suff)—though there were some more ambitious chapels at the end of the century.

The eighteenth century

The full force of Baroque was by no means exhausted with Wren. Several major architects worked within its tradition, and they included Thomas Archer and John James. Thomas Archer produced the fine churches of St. Philip's, Birmingham (W. Midlands), St. Paul's, Deptford, and St. John's, Westminster (London). John James designed St. George's, Hanover Square (London), and Whitchurch (London), which is richly adorned with paintings attributed to Louis Laguerre.

But foremost among the men who amplified the Baroque were Nicholas Hawksmoor and James Gibbs, who both rank as great architects. Hawksmoor had an audacious and original mind, capable at once of subtle detail and monumental breadth. His churches have a kind of barrelling power. There are six of them—half the number actually produced by the Act of Parliament of 1711 which called for fifty new London churches. They are: St. Alphege, Greenwich; St. Mary Woolnoth; St. George, Bloomsbury; and—all in Stepney—St. George's-in-the-East; Christ Church, Spitalfields (plate 15); and St. Anne, Limehouse.

More orthodox, and less emphatically Baroque than Hawksmoor's work, Gibbs's churches and other buildings are yet full of life, and marked by an admirable grace and richness. St. Mary-le-Strand is a beautifully compact and elegant building, and St. Martin-in-the-Fields (London) is a striking church which set a pattern both here and abroad. Other good churches by Gibbs are St. Peter's, Vere Street (London), All Saints, Derby, and St. Nicholas, Aberdeen.

Impressive churches were produced throughout the century, and many of them are listed in the gazetteer. Two of the more arresting ones are the circular church of St. Chad's, Shrewsbury (Salop), by George Steuart, and Great Witley (Worcs). This is in the rococo style, a diminutive and more light-hearted form of Baroque. It is resplendent with painted ceilings and white and gold plasterwork.

From about 1720 onwards, Palladian underwent a revival, led by the scholar and patron of the arts, Lord Burlington. But although the example of Inigo Jones was at last being assimilated, it was not assimilated without some change, and Palladian soon became the rather more tranquil style that prevailed throughout the Georgian period (1702-1830). Its benign influence was particularly apparent in domestic architecture, but it also resulted in some fine churches, including splendid Hardenhuish (Wilts) by John Wood of Bath, St Nicholas, Worcester, by Thomas White, and Blandford (Dorset) by William and John Bastard. These provincial architects made Palladian into a part of the English landscape.

From the 1760s onwards, however, there were various signs of change. Robert Adam modified Palladian by his more fanciful taste, Gothic was consciously revived, and buildings began to be modelled on the architecture of ancient Greece. Robert Adam's own style owed something to Greek and Pompeian feeling, as well as to Roman tradition, and is illustrated by his churches at Gunton (Norf), Mistley (Essex), and Binley (W. Midlands). His influence is apparent at All Hallows, London Wall, by George Dance Junior, and at Horbury (Yorks), by John Carr.

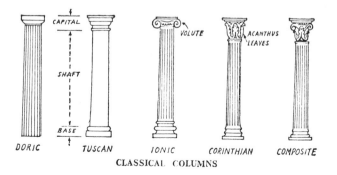

CLASSICAL COLUMNS

There had been an undercurrent of Gothic styles throughout the century, either in Classical adaptations, or in a natural continuation of country traditions. But now Gothic features were used as picturesque elements in a fantasia—though within a Classical framework, and with Classical fittings. This gave rise to the style known as Gothick or Neo-Gothic, and the buildings belonging to it can be very attractive, whether lucid and decorous as Francis Hiorne's church at Tetbury (Glos), romantic as Thorpe Market (Norf), or exotic and theatrical as Shobdon (Herefs)—which also draws strongly on the rococo and oriental styles then in fashion. Other examples include Croome (Worcs), Woolley (Avon), Stone (Staffs), Norton-by-Galby, Teigh and Stapleford (Leics), the secularized St. George's Episcopal Chapel, Edinburgh, by John Adam, and the ruinous Hartwell (Bucks).

The urbane severity of Greek architecture was introduced to England by James Stuart and Nicholas Revett. Although the style was not fully established until the Revival in the early years of the next century, Stuart demonstrated it at Nuneham Courtney (Oxon), and Revett at Ayot St. Lawrence (Herts), and from then on it was an influence to be reckoned with.

The Classical church architecture of Scotland is impressive. One thinks first of the major churches—St. Andrew's, Glasgow, by Allan Dreghorn; Gibbs's St. Nicholas, Aberdeen; Hamilton by William Adam, Robert Adam's father; and St. Andrew's, Edinburgh—the first church to be built in the Classical New Town of Edinburgh. But there are many other fine examples, including Montrose and St. Andrew's, Dundee (Angus), the High Kirk, Inverness, Cupar (Fife), Inveraray by Robert Mylne, and Fochabers (Aberdeens). Even early in the century, when not many churches were built, there were some good examples, as at Yester (E. Lothian), and Carrington (Midlothian). Small traditional churches were built throughout the period, though now with a Classical air—as at Golspie (Sutherland) and Glenbuchat (Aberdeens). Country churches tended to be long and narrow in the medieval manner, though the plan gradually became wider under Classical influence, as at Cults and Kirkhill (Inverness).

There is some Classical work in Welsh parish churches of the period, but the Established Church was declining, and most energy went into the creation of Nonconformist chapels. With their solemn biblical names such as Bethesda, Ebenezer, and Bethel, they are not to everyone's taste, but the more one sees of them, the more appealing they become. Various copybook elements, Classical or Gothic, are blended with originality and care by local builders, and now often have an air of deserted innocence. Good Nonconformist building is scattered throughout Wales, and in England fine examples are provided by the Octagon Chapel, Colegate, Norwich (Norf), and Wesley's Chapel (Bristol).

The nineteenth century

The Greek Revival was at its height from about 1810 to 1830. It produced some distinguished, if rather sober, churches. London has excellent examples in St. Pancras, by W. and H. W. Inwood, and St. Mary, St. Marylebone by Thomas Hardwick. Scottish architects took to this style with enthusiasm, especially for the façades of churches. It was as though Classicism in Scotland had finally found its most congenial form. Church after church went up—St. Mary's, Edinburgh, St. George's, Paisley (Renfrew), St. John's, Montrose (Angus), St. Leonard's, Perth, and best of all St. Giles, Elgin (Moray) and John Smith's North Kirk, Aberdeen. The Greek Revival lasted much longer in Scotland than in England, and its influence was still to be seen in Glasgow as late as the end of the century, as at St. George's-in-the-Fields. Soon after the middle of the century Alexander Thomson designed the imposing Caledonia Road Free Church, St. Vincent Street, and Queen's Park—all in his own eclectic manner.

Some of the Greek Revival churches, especially in London, were built in response to the Church Building Act of 1818. This applies to a few of the best examples, including the elegant All Souls, Langham Place (London), built by one of the Commissioners of the Act, John Nash. The three London churches built by another Commissioner, the idiosyncratic architect Sir John Soane, miss the brilliance of his best designs, but the Holy Trinity, Marylebone, for example, is a creditable piece of work. The sound achievements of other architects are well represented by churches such as St. George, Camberwell, and St. Mark, Kennington (London). There is still a slight surprise in seeing the temples of Ancient Greece set down in the gloomier suburbs of London.

But the Act had made provision for about 230 churches, to be built in the industrial Midlands and North, as well as in London. One million pounds was voted by Parliament for this purpose. Apart from the churches of the Greek Revival, few churches had been built in the last years of the eighteenth century and the early part of the nineteenth, but now that the Napoleonic wars were over, town populations were growing,

and the Industrial Revolution was upon Britain, a rapid pro-
gramme of building was necessary. The Commissioners'
Churches are only a small indication of the volume of building that followed, but they are still important. The reason is
that, although they could be in either Classic or Gothic
styles, so long as they were economical and spacious, most
of them were in Gothic—and this was a sign of the times.

Gothic was beginning to be taken far more seriously than
it had been in the eighteenth century, and some of the first
architects involved in its revival brought both ability and
integrity to their task. The result was churches such as St.
Peter, Brighton (Sussex) by Sir Charles Barry, St. Luke's,
Chelsea (London) by James Savage, Theale (Berks) by E.
Garbett, and St. Peter, Preston (Lancs) by Thomas Rickman.
All the same, these buildings still carry with them a sugges-
tion of Georgian coolness and grace, and while the ideal of
Gothic as the true Christian architecture may have been in the
air, it was the incandescent genius of Augustus Pugin that
finally ignited it in the Victorian mind.

Pugin, a convert to Roman Catholicism, had a deep admira-
tion for certain aspects of medieval civilization, and from the
time that he expressed his convictions in writing and in architecture, many people did not doubt that Gothic was both
structurally and spiritually superior to Classic. Pugin received
the support of influential groups such as the Ecclesiastical
Commission, the Oxford or Tractarian Movement, and the
Ecclesiologists of the Cambridge Camden Society. The revival
that followed had tremendous vitality, and although it gave
rise to some heavy and overcrowded work, it also produced
a great variety of original and admirable design.

In churches such as All Saints', Margaret Street (London),
William Butterfield cleverly used coloured brick, marble, and tile
as semi-precious substances, inlaying almost every surface with
them, until they merged into the vaulted gloom and greatly
enriched the mystery of interiors. But the ritual geometry of these
patterns was always cut through by an imperious use of line, and
while this ensured scale, it also imposed constraint. True
decorative liberality, though still tempered by structural and
dramatic considerations, belongs to the work of William Burges.
Burges designed Skelton and Studley Royal (Yorks), and his
natural sympathy with the jovial, graphic mind of the middle
ages makes his work very enjoyable. In spite of his intensity,
Pugin shared this visual sense of humour.

For purer virtues, and mastery over the techniques of

medieval masonry and vaulting, there was J. L. Pearson, whose best churches are St. Michael's, Croydon, St. John's Upper Norwood, St. Peter's, Vauxhall, and above all St. Augustine's, Kilburn (London). Pearson tended to favour the Early English style, whereas another architect of taste, G. F. Bodley, developed an extremely delicate version of Decorated, tending towards Perpendicular. George Street's work, on the other hand, was bold and dashing: it always has something adventurous and well-constructed to recommend it.

For sheer ability there was Sir Gilbert Scott, one of the great representative figures of the Gothic Revival. Apart from a mass of other projects, Scott worked on over 700 churches, often with far more sensitivity than he is given credit for—though he was also capabie of bold and grandiose work. His achievement is well represented by St. Giles, Camberwell (London).

For a dignified 'correctness' there was R. C. Carpenter; for churches conceived on an heroic scale, James Brooks—and for a sense of peace and mystery, there was Pugin himself. Peace is not something one would have associated with Pugin, whose energy was restless and consuming. But his fervour melted under the intensity of his art, and cooled to tranquillity. 'Peace and mystery' are not mere sentimental attributes. They depend upon the most exact aesthetic control—of line, of light and half-light, and of colour and ornament. Hardly any architects have been able to design such fine detail as Pugin, but he sometimes held this gift in abeyance, and produced churches imbued with simplicity. At other times his churches are emblazoned with the richest of decoration, and at St. Giles, Cheadle (Staffs) and finally at St. Augustine's, Ramsgate (Kent), Pugin realized one of his most compelling ideals—that of a remote medieval interior, hung with shadow and the glimmer of jewelled glass.

As well as all this work, there was a great deal of 'restoration'. Eighteenth century plaster ceilings were pulled down, plaster was scraped from the walls, and from 1840 onwards an effort was made to return churches to what they had been like before they were 'spoiled' in the seventeenth and eighteenth centuries, or even to recast them in the approved Decorated style. Restoration was sometimes very good, but more often it did great damage, and by the end of the century it was realized that what was needed was sympathetic preservation. Important changes were also made in the arrangement of interiors. Lecterns and ordinary seats were introduced, and the altar and chancel, complete with altar rails and choir stalls, were restored to prominence at the expense of the pulpit. These changes had the same purpose as the architecture of the period—to make religion awe-inspiring once again.

Gothic churches were still being built towards the end of the century, and many gifted architects did some work in this style. They include Norman Shaw, Sir William Emerson, Paley and Austin, who built the fine church of St. George, Stockport (Gtr Manchester), W. D. Caröe, who built St. David, Exeter (Devon), Basil Champneys, J. F. Bentley, J. D. Sedding, and his brother E. Sedding.

J. D. Sedding was an individualist: his church of the Holy Redeemer, Clerkenwell (London) is Italianate—and this is a reminder that not all Victorian churches, still less all Victorian buildings, were in the prevailing style. Three notable exceptions are the Lombardic Wilton (Wilts), the Roman Catholic Brompton Oratory (London), designed by Herbert Gribble in an Italian Baroque style, and the Belhaven-Westbourne Church, Glasgow.

With an architect such as Sedding, however, we are getting away from High Victorian Gothic, and the free Perpendicular of his church of the Holy Trinity, Sloane Street (London) is associated with the Arts and Crafts Movement of the 1880s. This movement, in which the designer William Morris played an important part, stressed the virtues of craftsmanship, simplicity, and harmony rather than those of strict historical accuracy—not that this had exercised any tyranny over the great Victorian architects.

The Arts and Crafts Movement did not abandon traditional forms, but it did modify them. There had always been architects such as E. B. Lamb, Sir William Tite, and Bassett Keeling, who objected to the 'official' Gothic, and they produced some strange, and sometimes successful churches in support of their views. But the Arts and Crafts Movement came as a more organized reaction against the Ecclesiologists' Gothic, and as its influence emerged in the Art Nouveau of the 1890s, it gave architecture not only an occasional simpering naïvety, but also the first notes of modernity.

The pattern of development in the nineteenth century was roughly the same for the whole country. The Classical style lingered on and produced churches such as Llanllwchaiarn (Powys), and St. Stephen's, Edinburgh.

Throughout the United Kingdom, the continuation of Classical traditions began to overlap with the first Gothic Revival churches—some of them, such as Kincardine-in-Menteith (Perths), and St. John's Episcopal Church, Edinburgh, among the most pleasant produced by the movement outside England. From that time on, there was a flood of Gothic work. It received early official encouragement from such things as the designs of Thomas Telford, the engineer, for the 42 churches allotted to the Highlands and Islands of Scotland by an Act of 1824. Iona (Argyll) is a good example of these Parliamentary Churches.

Some of the best Gothic Revival churches in Scotland and Wales are mentioned in the gazetteer. Those from the high and late Victorian periods include the Tolbooth Church, Edinburgh; Camphill-Queen's Park, Glasgow; Pearson's church at Llangasty-Talyllyn (Powys); and J. B. Fowler's at Bettws Disserth (Powys).

Many Nonconformist chapels were built in Wales, especially in the growing towns. Chapels could be simple gabled halls, but they eventually became large buildings—here as elsewhere, for Spurgeon's Tabernacle, Croydon (London) could hold 5,000 people.

The twentieth century

The rate of building that made the nineteenth century so remarkable was kept up in the first part of the twentieth century, to make provision for the rapidly expanding suburbs. A few good churches show the influence of the Arts and Crafts Movement, or of Art Nouveau. They include Kempley (Glos) by Randell Wells, Queen's Cross Church, Maryhill, Glasgow by C. R. Mackintosh, and above all St. Andrew, Roker (Tyne & Wear) by E. S. Prior. There were other original and eclectic designs, such as Sir Edwin Lutyens's St. Jude, Hampstead Garden Suburb (London), and P. M. Chalmers's Achnacarry, Dervaig, Mull (Argyll).

There were many more conventional churches, however, and most early twentieth century churches continue the tradition of Victorian Gothic, though the best of them especially tend towards an attenuated version of it. It is this that distinguishes the work of the outstanding church architects of the period—Sir Walter Tapper, Temple Moore, Sir Charles Nicholson, and Sir Ninian Comper. F. C. Eden did much first-rate work in restoring and furnishing churches. Comper designed the churches at Cosham (Hants), Carshalton (London), Wellingborough (Northants), and Kirriemuir (Angus). His work is particularly subtle in the way it blends Classic with Gothic, and uses pure forms as a foil for rich decoration—but all these men produced fine designs. It was a dignified end to a long tradition.

This was the tradition of building large and lavish churches. Churches now are simpler: congregations are smaller, ostentation would be out of place even if it could be paid for, and modern materials encourage uniformity. Most of the outstanding recent churches are foreign, and when we are not providing utility buildings, we seem to specialize in decoration. But all this is no reason why churches should be mediocre—and many of them are as dull, smug, and featureless as factories. Some of the efforts to avoid this have resulted only in a modish engineering rigour and brittle good taste. Others have been more fortunate, and in arriving at a light, cool balance they have contributed something at least to British church building tradition.

4. LOCAL CHARACTERISTICS AND MATERIALS

Several kinds of stone are found in Britain, and each one tends to bring with it certain architectural features. One of the main kinds is the limestone that occurs in the sweep of country embracing Yorkshire, Lincolnshire, Derbyshire, Nottinghamshire, Leicestershire, Northamptonshire, Bedfordshire, Oxfordshire, Gloucestershire, Wiltshire, and Somerset. In the middle ages, limestone was quarried at such places as Tadcaster (Yorks), Barnack (Cambs), and Doulting (Som), and had to be carried by waterway to Norfolk, other parts of Cambridgeshire, and south Lincolnshire. Limestone lasts well and is suitable for fine carving. It therefore gives to all these areas their great churches, rich in detail, and often completed by soaring spires, as in the splendid churches of the Nene valley in Northamptonshire. Other counties containing good spires are Staffordshire, Warwickshire, Cornwall, Devon, and Herefordshire. A form of limestone known as Kentish rag was often used for church walls in Kent, and since stone is rare in Essex, Kentish rag was sometimes imported across the Thames estuary.

The local granite lends austerity to the fifteenth century churches of Cornwall, though there is an exception in the profuse carved decoration of Launceston. Sandstone, on the other hand, is a soft stone, warm in colour and easily carved into intricate shapes, though these wear away with time. All this gives a mellow richness to the churches of Cheshire, Shropshire, Herefordshire, and parts of Lancashire, Staffordshire, Warwickshire, and Worcestershire.

In areas such as Wales and Cumbria stone was used in a rather rough-and-ready way to make churches without the distinction of any one period, but still possessing a strong attraction in their setting. The same applies to the many small stone churches scattered throughout the country, and forming a constant background to more fitful and ambitious efforts.

SAXON LONG AND SHORT CORNER WORK   RUBBLE WALL   RANDOM COURSING   ASHLAR   STONE AND FLINT CHEQUERS

TYPES OF MASONRY

Another very common material is flint, which was much used in counties such as Suffolk, Norfolk, and Essex, where there is almost no stone suitable for carving. The most elaborate use of flint is in the flushwork of East Anglia, but flint also gives character to many churches in Buckinghamshire, Hertfordshire, south Oxfordshire, Berkshire, Wiltshire, Hampshire, Surrey, and south Sussex and Kent.

The chalk often found with flint was also occasionally employed in building.

Surrey, Essex, Hampshire, Berkshire, Shropshire, Herefordshire, and the border counties of Wales all tend to lack good building stone. In these areas, particularly in Essex, wood and brick are very common building materials, and the small churches made of them are often very pleasant. Apart from its extensive use in Saxon times, wood was hardly used for anything except roofs and porches until the Perpendicular period. Wooden porches are common in Essex, Sussex, and Surrey: at Lurgashall (Sussex) there is a wooden cloister, and North Fambridge (Essex) has a wooden narthex.

Not all Perpendicular towers were splendid stone structures, and many belfries and bell-towers were built in wood. They were often topped by a shingled spire, and this form is characteristic of Essex, Surrey, Hampshire, and Kent. Pyramid-shaped tower roofs are also found in these counties

—though they are so common in Sussex that they are sometimes known as 'Sussex heads' or 'caps'. Roofs of pyramidal form, though broken by a louvre-stage and clad in tile or slate, are found in Shropshire, Powys and Gwent. Brookland (Kent) has a detached timber belfry with a conical cap.

Wood only provided the framework of taller spires: the covering was of lead or, later, of copper. The slender leaded 'spike' already mentioned as typical of Hertfordshire is also found in East Anglia. Quite often, in all the counties mentioned, there is no tower and spire, but a small bell-cote instead —and this can be very effective. Half-timber work is found in counties near the Welsh border such as Shropshire and Cheshire. Additional use of wood was sometimes made in arcades.

The Saxons used Roman brick in such areas as Hertfordshire, Essex, and Surrey, but there was little building in brick after that until the Perpendicular and Tudor periods. Many examples of this later building occur in the counties originally mentioned, but there are also a few examples in Buckinghamshire, Kent, Suffolk, Hertfordshire, Sussex, and Norfolk. The parts most often made of brick are the tower and the porch.

The Victorians were very keen on polychrome, but apart from that, marble polychrome was used in the middle ages, especially in the Early English period, as at Arreton (Isle of Wight). The most important sources of marble were Petworth (Sussex), Bethersden (Kent), and the Purbeck district of Dorset. Ordinary local stones of different colours were used to make designs in several churches in Northamptonshire, Leicestershire, Bedfordshire, and Cornwall. A chequered pattern, often of flint and stone, or brick, occurs at a few places, such as Luton (Beds), and Bere Regis (Dorset). Cross-shaped patterns in coloured brick, and diaperwork consisting of square or lozenge shapes are both features of some East Anglian and Essex churches.

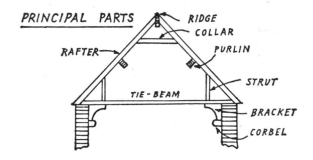

PRINCIPAL PARTS — RIDGE — COLLAR — RAFTER — PURLIN — STRUT — TIE-BEAM — BRACKET — CORBEL

TIMBER ROOF STRUCTURES

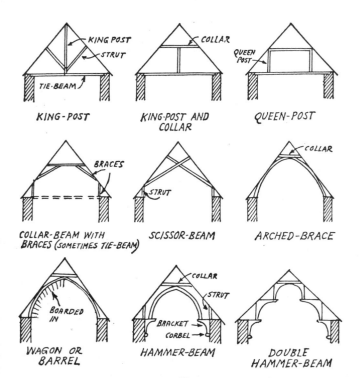

KING-POST

KING-POST AND COLLAR

QUEEN-POST

COLLAR-BEAM WITH BRACES (SOMETIMES TIE-BEAM)

SCISSOR-BEAM

ARCHED-BRACE

WAGON OR BARREL

HAMMER-BEAM

DOUBLE HAMMER-BEAM

53

5. FEATURES AND FITTINGS

Woodwork

Roofs

Stone vaults are generally found in larger parish churches, and most churches have timber roofs. There were many different types of these, and they were often made with great craftsmanship. Aisles were usually roofed with plain beams supported by braces fixed to the wall. Main roofs were gabled, and the various parts are shown on page 53.

The strengthening devices that give roofs their distinctive names and styles were not usually provided for every single rafter, or common rafter, but only for the principal rafters, which usually mark the internal bays of the church. The common rafter might, however, be strengthened by some lighter and less elaborate kind of device. The rafters rested on a wall-plate, or timber running along the top of the wall.

Norman roofs were simple structures filled in by a truss or framework of timbers supported on oak tie-beams. The fact that they were simple does not mean that they were uninteresting: the simplest roofs, in any period, can be among the most satisfactory. The more elaborate, open form of roofing was not developed until the thirteenth century, and did not reach its fullest complexity until the Perpendicular period—when the wagon-roof and the hammer-beam roof in particular became established as two of the most impressive achievements of British church builders.

At the same time, roofs in general were becoming far more shallow, after the extreme pitch of the thirteenth century, and as the gap between tie-beam and rafter narrowed it might be filled with a spandrel, which could be pierced with tracery. In addition, tie-beams might be cambered, and in the fifteenth century some roofs were so flat that the rafters rested on the tie-beams, which were painted or carved.

A few hammer-beam roofs were built in the later part of the Perpendicular period, but from the Restoration onwards, plaster ceilings were the rule, and their designs can be extremely elegant. There are good examples at King Charles the Martyr, Tunbridge Wells (Kent), Ingestre (Staffs), Euston (Suff), and Great Witley (Worcs).

Some of the roofs shown on page 53 were common—the arched-brace was, for example—but others, such as the scissor-beam, were rare. The wagon-roof—so called because of its resemblance to the canvas cover of a wagon—is often found in the West Country. In this type of roof the common rafters, as well as the principal ones, are given arched-braces—and these may be left bare, or else 'ceiled' with a covering of plaster or boards.

Ceiled roofs were frequently divided into plain, flat panels, or into sunken ones carved with bosses and mouldings, and painted and gilded. There are magnificent examples at Hartland and Cullompton (Devon), and one of later date at Muchelney (Som). Sometimes only the area above the rood was panelled and adorned—as at Hennock (Devon)—and this canopy is known as a celure. There is a splendid example, this time on a hammer-beam roof, at Southwold (Suff).

Hammer-beam roofs are typical of East Anglia. Occasionally, hammer-beams were alternated with arched-braces, or else with tie-beams—as in the outstanding case of Mildenhall (Suff). But more often, hammer-beam roofs were unified creations, painted and gilded, and even decorated with flights of angels. This was an inspired invention, whether it appears in single hammer-beam roofs, as at Cawston and South Creake (Norf), or—in the most marvellous instances of all—in double hammer-beam roofs. There are fine examples at Swaffham (Norf), Woolpit (Suff), and March (Cambs), which has over a hundred angels.

Doors

In Saxon and early medieval times, doors were stout defences made of planks, and ornament, when it became fashionable, was provided by the reinforcing ironwork. But in the Decorated and Perpendicular periods, doors were frequently embellished with tracery, which was either carved in the fabric of the door itself or, later, applied in the form of cut-out mouldings, as at Stoke-by-Nayland (Suff) and St. Nicholas, King's Lynn (Norf).

Seating and lofts

Carved woodwork is one of the outstanding features of British churches, and reached a particular mastery in the fifteenth century, though hardly any pre-Reformation examples remain in Ireland and Scotland.

Bench-ends were often beautifully carved in the fifteenth and sixteenth centuries, especially in East Anglia and the West Country. The West Country type is square-headed, and there are fine examples at Launceston, Talland, and Launcells (Cornwall), Broomfield (Som), and High Bickington (Devon). Many East Anglian bench-ends, on the other hand, are completed by poppyheads, or finials carved in the form of figures, heads, grotesques, animals, or foliage. There are excellent series at Ufford, Dennington, Woolpit, Blythburgh, and Fressingfield (Suff), St. Mary, and St. German, Wiggenhall, and Ranworth (Norf), Tideswell (Derbys), and Great Brington (Northants).

Another distinction is possible, which does not depend on district: bench-ends can either be traceried, or else carved with figures, as at Haverfordwest (Dyfed), or other pictorial subjects, as at Altarnun (Cornwall), Bishop's Lydeard and East Brent (Som), and Lapford, Abbotsham, and East Budleigh (Devon). Not all bench-ends were so rich, even in the fifteenth century, and earlier ones were left plain. Their heads were either square, or in the fourteenth century simply shaped, as at Clapton in Gordano (Avon) and Dunsfold (Surrey).

A few places have choir or chancel stalls, some of them with intricate canopies—as at Whalley, and St. Mary, Lancaster (Lancs), Cartmel (Cumbria), All Saints, Hereford, Nantwich (Ches), Wensley (Yorks), Newark (Notts), Ludlow (Salop), and King's College Chapel, Aberdeen. Other examples are less ornate, but still fine, as at Wingfield (Suff) and Tong (Salop).

Stalls were sometimes given additional decoration in the form of elbows and misericords. Elbows are the projections between stalls carved with figures, animals, or grotesques, as at Nantwich (Ches) and Southwold (Suff). Misericords are shelving projections on the under side of the hinged seats in choir stalls. When the seat was turned up, the misericord gave support to the person standing. The 'shelf' itself was supported by a bracket, which was carved with such things as animals, foliage, emblems, heads—as at Balsham (Cambs)—or with various scenes, as at Lavenham (Suff), Ludlow (Salop), and Whalley (Lancs). There are other good examples at Gresford (Clwyd).

Sometimes a prominent local family wanted benches kept for private use, and the name of their house was inscribed on the back of the benches, or seats were reserved in the chancel. Then, in the Renaissance, family pews came into being, and by the eighteenth century they had developed into substantial panelled structures, complete with coloured baize linings, and even with stoves or fireplaces, stairs and hatpegs. Pews such as these, enclosed and given a canopy, are known as box pews. At first they belonged to the squire, but in the eighteenth century the congregation, too, was allowed box pews, though often without the canopies. These various types of pew are generally very well made. A few Scottish churches, such as Pitsligo (Aberdeens), Kilbirnie (Ayrs), and Lecropt (Perths) retain fine 'laird's lofts' ranging in date from the seventeenth to nineteenth centuries. Ayr has lofts for sailors, traders, and merchants, and Burntisland (Fife) has a sailors' loft and magistrates' pew.

Pulpits and lecterns

Wooden pulpits began to be a feature of churches in the fifteenth century, and most were octagonal. They were carved with tracery, and sometimes decorated with figures. These were either painted, as in several Norfolk churches, or else carved and set in canopied niches, as at Minehead, and in the splendid example at Trull (Som). The richest carving was in the pulpits of Somerset and Devon, which has good examples at Dartmouth, Kenton (plate 18), Ipplepen, Torbryan, and Bovey Tracey.

Very occasionally, a fifteenth century pulpit will be surmounted by a tester, or sounding-board, as at Edlesborough (Bucks). Testers were more common by the seventeenth century, and many impressive pulpits remain from this period, as well as some simple but pleasant ones. There are particularly fine examples at Abbotsbury (Dorset), Croscombe (Som), Brancepeth (Durham), St. John, Leeds (Yorks), St. Clement, King William Street (London), Ingestre (Staffs), St. Mary Walbrook (London), St. Columba's, and Elgin (Moray).

Impressive pulpits dating from the eighteenth century may be found at Croome (Worcs), Wanstead (London), and Golspie (Sutherland), for example. By this time pulpits were sometimes two-decker, as at Avington (Hants), and quite often three-decker, combining clerk's seat, lectern, and pulpit and tester. In the sixteenth and seventeenth centuries, pulpits were fitted with hour-glasses and stands, so that sermons could be timed.

A few medieval wooden lecterns remain. Lecterns were often of the desk type, facing two ways, and sometimes having two levels, one for kneeling, the other for standing. Occasionally lecterns were carved in the shape of an eagle—a pattern very popular for brass lecterns in the middle ages, and ever since.

Interiors after the Reformation

The royal arms introduced by Henry VIII are often found in churches, whether carved and set in place of the rood, painted on walls or panels, or worked in stained glass or embroidery. From the time of Elizabeth onwards, they were flanked under the chancel arch by panels bearing the Ten Commandments and the Lord's Prayer. Later on the Decalogue was often set in a Classical reredos.

Hatchments—memorial boards painted with the arms of the dead person—were hung in churches from the seventeenth century onwards. Lettered boards giving details of charitable bequests are also common.

Throughout the middle ages, the music in churches had been provided by simple forms of organ. But these were destroyed by the Puritans, and after this, choirs were accompanied by string and woodwind orchestras situated in the west galleries which had been built from the time of Elizabeth onwards. The old instruments such as bassoons and oboes have sometimes been kept by parish churches. Organs were reinstalled in the seventeenth and eighteenth centuries, often in the galleries, and a few churches have barrel organs. Organs were fitted with carved cases. The only surviving medieval organ-case is the one at Old Radnor (Powys), dating from 1500, but many equally splendid examples remain from the seventeenth and eighteenth centuries, as at St. Magnus the Martyr, London Bridge, St. Peter, Cornhill, and St. Mary Woolnoth (London).

Three-sided altar rails, sometimes made of wrought iron, were put in churches throughout the seventeenth century and on into the eighteenth as a result of Laud's influence. The Communion table itself may be a fine piece of Elizabethan, Jacobean, or eighteenth century furniture, as at St. John's (Bristol) and Wheatfield (Oxon). Some chancels contain bishop's chairs dating from the seventeenth century.

Everything about seventeenth and eighteenth century interiors combined to give a well-furnished feeling to churches —even down to the occasional use of wall-panelling, as in the seventeenth century example at North Molton (Devon).

First-rate seventeenth century interiors complete with contemporary fittings are to be found in many London and other city churches, and at Croscombe (Som), St. John, Leeds (Yorks), Puddletown (Dorset), Leighton Bromswold (Cambs), Groombridge (Kent), Euston (Suff), Sedgefield (Durham), and Ayr.

From the eighteenth century come the churches and fittings of Avington (Hants), Gayhurst (Bucks), All Saints, Oxford, and Chiselhampton (Oxon), Badminton (Avon), Castle

Bromwich (W. Midlands), St. Swithin, Worcester, and Norton-by-Galby (Leics).

Altars and retables

In Saxon times the altar was wooden, but from the eleventh century to the Reformation it was made of stone. This form is called a mensa, and its top was marked with five small crosses, which were anointed by the consecrating bishop, and which stood for the Five Wounds of Christ. Some stone altars had a small hollow fashioned in them so that they could contain the relic of a saint. Altars were covered with embroidered cloths, frontals, and side-curtains, or riddels. Other embroidery can be seen in vestments such as copes.

Instead of a reredos, an altar might be given a retable, or altar-piece. This could be an embroidered fabric, but usually it was wooden, and in this case it was carved and painted, and often triptych-shaped—though fourteenth century retables with five, seven, or more panels are known. There are good examples at Withyham (Sussex), St. Michael-at-Plea, Norwich (Norf), and Thornton Parva (Suff). Occasionally the altar was constructed in the form of a chest, and then the upturned lid acted as a retable.

Chests, boxes, aumbries, and sacrament houses

Many churches have chests, which were used to store money, vestments, or documents such as parish registers. Parish registers record much of the social life of this country from the sixteenth century onwards. Some chests have interesting carving, iron locks, and bindings. Among the various kinds of boxes to be found in churches are Bible boxes, collection boxes, and alms boxes or poor boxes.

Aumbries are cupboards in the north wall of the chancel, where sacred vessels and oils were kept. Aumbry doors have generally disappeared, but the recesses are often still there. The Scottish version of these cupboards, dating from the fifteenth and sixteenth centuries, is the sacrament house, and there are good examples at Deskford (Banffs) and Crichton (Midlothian). The bread that was given to the poor as a result of bequests was kept in ventilated cupboards called dole-cupboards, though the same purpose was sometimes served by bread-shelves.

Font-covers

The font stands near the main door at the western end of the church. In order to stop people stealing the holy water for medicinal or superstitious purposes, fonts were given covers from the thirteenth century onwards. At first these were flat, and secured by iron bands, locks—and staples, which may remain attached to fonts.

By the fifteenth century, however, more varied forms of cover had been devised. Triptych cupboards with locking doors were sometimes fixed on top of fonts. The font at Thaxted (Essex) is completely encased in a wooden structure, and at Trunch and St. Peter Mancroft, Norwich (Norf) the fonts are provided with canopies set on carved posts and made so as to receive the cover when it was raised.

The most splendid covers of the period are tall, spire-like crowns of the sort found at Sall (Norf), and carved with pinnacles, tabernacle-work, and tracery. The usual arrangement for lifting these covers was a pulley and cable with counterweight attached, but occasionally the lowest stage can be raised in telescopic fashion—as at Ufford and Sudbury (Suff). Other graceful examples are to be found at Halifax, and St. Peter, Bradford (Yorks), St. Andrew, Newcastle (Tyne & Wear), Barking, Woodbridge, and Hepworth (Suff), Ewelme (Oxon), North Walsham (Norf), and—from the seventeenth century—at Astbury (Ches), Brancepeth and Haughton-le-Skerne (Durham). The last two churches belong to a group of several in County Durham fitted with 'Cosin' woodwork—that is woodwork installed by John Cosin, ' a churchman of the school of Laud' and eventually Bishop of Durham. Most of these elaborate font-covers, however, are found in East Anglia. After the Restoration, covers were simpler and smaller, and were often given an ogee shape.

Screens

Like many other fittings in the middle ages, screens were painted, and this must have added greatly to the effect of interiors. The first examples of wooden screens date from the thirteenth century and imitate the styles of slightly earlier stone screens. As screens increased in number in the fourteenth century, this influence was shed, and several distinct types of screen emerged, culminating in the immense variety and wealth of fifteenth century screen-carving. East Anglian screens have an air of reserve, and are light and graceful, with square-headed bays, and shallow rood-lofts jutting straight out—though not all screens had lofts. There are good examples at Dennington (Suff) and South Creake (Norf).

West Country screens are low, wide, and densely decorated. They have deep gallery fronts supported by vaulting, and ornamented with openwork bands. The result is a cheerful opulence that can be almost cloying at times. Some of the most spectacular examples are in Devon, as at Kentisbeare, Cullompton, Atherington, Ipplepen, and Lapford. Both East Anglian and Devon screens sometimes have figures of saints painted in the lower panels, for example, as at Ranworth (Norf) and Plymtree (Devon).

In Welsh screen-design, tracery and openwork bands are piled high in patterns as rich and intricate as lace. This kind of work is often found in Powys, as at Llananno, Llanegryn, Partrishow and Llanwnog, though fine examples also occur at Llanrwst (Gwynedd), and at St. Margaret's (Herefs).

These remarks do not cover every case. Since the square-headed and restrained type of screen is the most basic kind, it is found in many areas apart from East Anglia, especially in the Midlands, as at Higham Ferrers (Northants). Screens in the Midlands and North are hard to classify, though one can detect some types, such as the square-headed screens with ogee tracery and tabernacling found in Yorkshire, as at Flamborough. Good examples of other kinds of screen are to be found at Astbury and Mobberley (Ches), Hillesden (Bucks), Aymestrey (Herefs), Campsall (Yorks), Hexham (Northumb), Coates-by-Stow (Lincs)—and, from the sixteenth century, at Sutton-on-Trent (Notts), the Chapel of King's College, Aberdeen, and Foulis Easter (Perths). There is excellent Cosin screenwork at Sedgefield (Durham).

The staircase leading to the roodloft was usually set in the wall at the end of the screen, but occasionally it was built as a projecting turret, as in the beautiful example at Totnes (Devon). Parclose screens generally belong to the Perpendicular period, and many of them contain excellent work, as at Cirencester (Glos), Barking (Suff), and Mere (Wilts). Renaissance screens were often handsome, and apart from the splendid choir screen at Abbey Dore (Herefs), and the parclose screens at St. John, Cardiff (Glam), there are fine rood screens at Holdenby (Northants), Ingestre (Staffs), Cholmondeley (Ches), and St. Paul's, Waldenbury (Herts). Some Victorian and Edwardian architects were very good at restoring old screens and designing new ones. The work of F. C. Eden, G. F. Bodley, Sir Walter Tapper, Sir Charles Nicholson, and Sir Ninian Comper is particularly distinguished.

Fittings in stone

Fonts

Saxon fonts are rare, but a large number of fonts have survived from the Norman period, when they became regular features in churches. Most Norman fonts are made of stone, and the basic kind is a round bowl, though this was often placed on a pedestal, or on a pedestal and four corner-shafts. Pedestal fonts occasionally have square bowls.

The more primitive fonts were left plain, but it is the decorative carving that makes Norman fonts so distinct as a class. This carving frequently contains a grotesque element, while many Welsh fonts show the enduring influence of Celtic work. Decoration in general ranges from patterns of interlace or symbol, to designs involving emblematic creatures such as the Four Evangelists, and finally to figure-compositions that deserve the name of sculpture. These represent biblical scenes, the figures or Lives of Saints, or else symbolic figures such as those standing for the Seven Virtues—Faith, Hope, Charity, Prudence, Justice, Fortitude, and Temperance. The carving is bold and shows great feeling for design and the play of light and shade. It is a considerable artistic achievement—strong, dramatic, and not to be overshadowed by subsequent refinements. It is the same achievement that we see in pieces of figure-sculpture such as the one in the porch at Malmesbury (Wilts).

There are good examples of carved Norman fonts at Stottesdon (Salop), Castle Frome, Eardisley, and Shobdon (Herefs), Llanarth and Llanfair-Clydogau (Dyfed), Avington (Berks), St. Mary, Stafford, St. Nicholas, Brighton (Sussex), Tintagel (Cornwall), Cenarth (Dyfed), and Llanwrthwl (Powys).

As well as these typical kinds of Norman font, there are several special kinds. Black marble from Tournai in Belgium was used to make a very impressive form of pedestal font. There are only five in parish churches—at East Meon, St. Mary Bourne, and St. Michael, Southampton (Hants), St. Peter, Ipswich (Suff), and Thornton Curtis (Humber). Fonts were sometimes made of cast lead in medieval times. Many of the best examples—some of them ornamented with figures and arcading—are Norman, as at Dorchester (Oxon), Warham (Norf), Frampton-on-Severn (Glos), Brookland (Kent), and Edburton (Sussex). Other special types of Norman font are found in west Dyfed, and in the areas around Aylesbury (Bucks), and Bodmin and Launceston (Cornwall). Norman

SAXON

NORMAN

LATE
NORMAN

EARLY ENGLISH

PERPENDICULAR
WITH PINNACLED
COVER

DECORATED WITH 'OGEE' COVER

CLASSICAL

FONTS

fonts are fairly common in Wales generally. They are rarer in Scotland, but there are examples at Linton (Roxburgh) and Birnie (Moray).

It was unnecessary to make many fonts in the thirteenth and fourteenth centuries. The relatively few examples remaining are more slender than Norman fonts, and have smaller bowls. Many are octagonal, and this continued to be a standard shape in the fifteenth century. Font decoration in the thirteenth and fourteenth centuries concentrated on architectural forms such as arcading, mouldings, and carved foliage. By the end of the fourteenth century, however, figure-carving had begun to return, and many of the most impressive fifteenth century fonts are carved with angels, saints, or figures representing the Seven Sacraments—Baptism, Confirmation, the Eucharist, Penance, Ordination, Marriage, and Extreme Unction. Most 'Seven Sacrament' fonts are in Norfolk, as at East Dereham, and in Suffolk, as at Great Glemham. Biblical scenes, heraldic subjects, the symbols of the Four Evangelists, and quatrefoils contained in panels also provided popular forms of decoration. The best fifteenth century examples are elegantly proportioned and carved.

The Renaissance brought with it a new type of font—a diminutive bowl set upon a Classical pedestal, and often ornamented with the cherubs' heads characteristic of the age. This type is particularly common in the City churches, but there are similar fonts at Willen (Bucks) and Castle Bromwich (W. Midlands), for example. Sometimes the basin was set on a bracket attached to the altar rails or pulpit: this was originally the case with the graceful examples at Teigh (Leics). A few wooden fonts remain—Norman at Efenechty (Clwyd); Perpendicular at Marks Tey (Essex); Renaissance at Christ Church (Bristol); and eighteenth century in the superb example at Croome (Worcs).

Screens

Although most rood-screens were made of wood, a fair number of stone ones survive from the fourteenth and fifteenth centuries, when they were painted in the same way as wooden screens. The basic design consisted of three arched openings, as in the beautiful screen at Bottisham (Cambs). Sometimes these openings were simply 'cut' in the chancel wall, while at Great Bardfield and Stebbing (Essex) the main chancel-arch is filled with stone tracery in the manner of a three-light window.

11. Long Melford (Suffolk): another of the 'wool churches' of the late fifteenth century, although the tower was built in 1903.

12. Great Coxwell (Oxfordshire): the tithe barn, used for storing the clergy's share, a tenth, of all local produce.

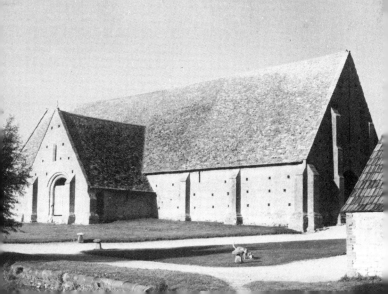

13. *St James Garlickhithe, London: one of Sir Christopher Wren's City churches in the Classical style of the seventeenth century.*

14. West Wycombe (Buckinghamshire): St Lawrence's church, built in the eighteenth century, is famous for the golden ball at the top of the tower, a prominent landmark.

15. Christ Church, Spitalfields, London: an example of Nicholas Hawksmoor's work in the eighteenth-century Classical style.

16. St Albans, Hertfordshire: St Michael's church has Anglo-Saxon nave and chancel, twelfth-century aisles, fifteenth-century nave roof and font and seventeenth-century pulpit, and a monument to Sir Francis Bacon.

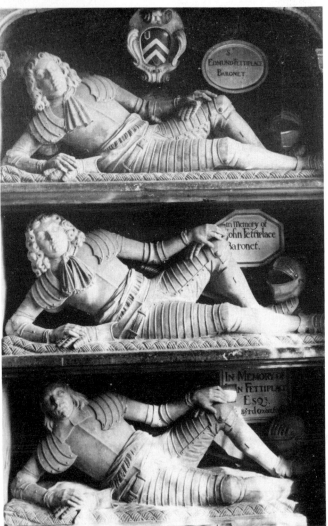

Text visible on tombs:
S EDMUND FETIPLACE BARONET

In Memory of John Fettirlace Baronet.

IN MEMORY OF N FETTIPLACE ESQ: b:rd Oxonfo

17. Swinbrook, Oxfordshire: the church of St Mary the Virgin is renowned for the tombs of the Fettiplace family, who flourished in Tudor and Stuart times.

18. (Right) Kenton, Devon: the fine carved pulpit.

ENTER INTO HIS GATES WITH THANKSGIVING
AND INTO HIS COURTS WITH PRAISE.

19. Rottingdean, East Sussex: the lychgate at the entrance to the churchyard.

Gradually the basic design was elaborated, until we get such fine fifteenth century screens as those at Totnes (Devon) and Compton Bassett in Wiltshire—which has more stone screens than any other county. There is a splendid sixteenth century example in Beer stone at Awliscombe (Devon), and other good stone screens at Roslin (Midlothian), and Llantwit Major (Glam). Parclose screens were also occasionally made of stone.

Pulpits

Only sixty stone pulpits survive, and they date from the late fourteenth century onwards. Eleven of them are in Devon, as at Dittisham and Harberton, and some of them are excellent pieces of work, the main form of decoration being cusped panelling. Later on, however, the decoration sometimes consisted of figures set in niches, as at South Molton (Devon).

Reredoses and alabaster panels

Most stone reredoses were destroyed during the Reformation. They depicted such things as the Passion of Christ, the Life of the Virgin Mary, and the figures of the Apostles. The subjects were set in panels or canopied niches. Chapel altars were sometimes given reredoses, as at St. Cuthbert, Wells (Som). Complete reredoses remain at Bampton and Somerton (Oxon), and Drayton (Oxon), and fragments at Linlithgow (W. Lothian)—old reredoses being almost non-existent in Scotland. Coloured and gilded, reredoses must once have been among the splendours of church interiors.

In the fourteenth and fifteenth centuries, many reredoses were made of alabaster, or gypsum, quarried in Derbyshire. Small pictorial panels of alabaster were carved at centres such as London and York, and widely distributed, for use in tombs as well as in reredoses. Subjects included the Lives and Martyrdoms of Saints, and the Last Judgement, in addition to those already mentioned. Although these panels were produced in some quantities, they were also works of art, as is shown by the examples at Lydiate (Lancs), St. Elphin, Warrington (Ches), Harewood (Yorks), Willoughby (Lincs), Minster Lovell (Oxon), and Long Melford (Suff). Some churches have statues made of alabaster, and at Kidwelly (Dyfed) there is one dating from the fourteenth century, and representing the Virgin and Child.

Tiles

Encaustic tiles are among the more obscure features of churches, though good examples were produced in the thirteenth and fifteenth centuries. They were made by stamping designs in red fireclay, filling the impress with white slip, covering with lead glaze, and firing until the slip turned yellow. Tiles depict scenes or heraldic devices, and individual tiles were often designed as elements of a larger unit. An alternative way of making tiles was to draw or scrape the design through a coating of slip. Encaustic tiles were very popular in Victorian times, and when used without discretion, they gave interiors a lurid gloss.

Fittings in metal

Door furniture

Metal was never as important as wood and stone for church fittings, and anyhow most medieval metalwork has disappeared. Many doors dating from the twelfth century onwards, however, are decorated with wrought-iron hinges, handles, knockers, and locks. Early Norman hinges recall Viking designs, as at Stillingfleet (Yorks), and the main hinges were usually crescent-shaped. After this, they became more geometrical for a while, as in the twelfth century example at Skipwith (Yorks), but by the thirteenth century a very graceful kind of scrollwork had been developed, which was also used to decorate chests. It is very well seen in the doors of Worksop (Notts) and Eaton Bray and Turvey (Beds). The hinges at the last two churches are by Thomas de Leighton, the most famous smith of the period.

When decorative wooden tracery started to replace scrollwork in the fourteenth century, smiths concentrated on lockplates, door-handles, and knockers. These may be fine pieces of design—they are on the doors of St. Nicholas, Gloucester, and Stoke Lyne (Oxon), for example—and as before, similar work was sometimes used to secure and adorn chests, as at Crediton (Devon) and East Dereham (Norf).

Tomb-railings

Although medieval wrought-iron grilles or screens survive in a few cathedrals, there are none in parish churches. Medieval tomb-railings or grates occasionally remain, however, and these fourteenth century innovations were designed to enclose the altar or table tombs then becoming fashionable.

The railings were made of iron or bronze, and there are examples at Bunbury (Ches) and West Tanfield (Yorks) in the form of hearses, with prickets or spikes for holding candles. But the chief examples are at Farleigh Hungerford (Som), and in the Beauchamp Chapel at Warwick. The grate at Farleigh Hungerford typifies the fashion for sawn ironwork that arose in the fourteenth century.

Screens

Metalwork underwent a renaissance in the seventeenth and eighteenth centuries, and many screens and gates adorning chancels and chapels date from this period. Among the masters of the craft were William Edney of Bristol, John and Robert Davies of Wrexham, and Robert Bakewell of Derby. It is to these men that we owe the superb work at St. Mary Redcliffe, St. Nicholas, and the Lord Mayor's Chapel (Bristol), Malpas (Ches), Ruthin, and Wrexham (Clwyd), Staunton Harold (Leics), and All Saints, Derby.

Altar tables, rails, etc.

A wide range of fittings was made in metal from the Renaissance onwards. It includes altar tables, as at St. Mary, Beverley (Humber), altar rails, as at Binley and Castle Bromwich (W. Midlands), mace-rests, and sword-rests, as at All Saints, Worcester. Candelabra exist from the middle ages onwards, as at St. John, Perth, and graceful seventeenth and eighteenth century examples made of brass are still common. Clocks were in use as early as the twelfth century, but were not given dials until at least the fourteenth century. Instead, mechanical figures called jacks might be used to tell the time by striking bells. One can sometimes see examples of the arms and armour which churchwardens had to look after for the militia.

Church plate

Medieval church plate is rare. Since it is often made of precious materials such as silver, gold, jewels and enamel, it is now locked up for safety. Medieval plate includes the chalice, pyx, monstrance, paten, christmatory, and cruets, as well as the holy water sprinkler, processional cross, sacring bell, censer, pax, alms dishes, and candlesticks. The pyx, containing the host, was raised and lowered by a pulley set in the ceiling. After the Reformation, the Communion cup was substituted for the chalice, and flagons, often made of pewter, were used instead of cruets. Some splendid plate remains from Victorian times.

Memorial brasses

A brass is a plate, engraved with a figure representing the person commemorated, and set flush in a stone indent—often in a place now hidden by a mat, pew, or other fitting. The metal used was an alloy of copper and zinc called latten and the engraving was done with a burin. The drawing often shows great feeling for line and pattern, and though the quality declined from the sixteenth century onwards, there are some good sixteenth century examples, as at Hever (Kent) and Winwick (Ches). The figure depicted was usually a stock one, but a few brasses present a likeness, as at Stoke-by-Nayland (Suff). There are about 4,000 brasses in Britain—the earliest example being the thirteenth century one at Stoke d'Abernon (Surrey), and the later ones dating from the seventeenth and eighteenth centuries.

Brasses provide an excellent historical source, especially since they show developments in armour and civilian dress from the thirteenth to the seventeenth centuries. The main centres of production were in the trading areas of the country —London and the Home Counties, East Anglia, and the West Country. As a result, merchants were increasingly commem-orated, particularly in the fifteenth century, as at Ipswich (Suffolk), Mereworth (Kent), and Taplow (Bucks). Brasses to wool-merchants are common in the Chilterns, the Lincoln-shire Wolds, and the Cotswolds, as at Northleach (Glos).

But many brasses commemorated noblemen, who were usually shown wearing armour. There are good examples at Trumpington (Cambs)—thirteenth century, Westley Waterless (Cambs) and Cobham (Kent)—fourteenth century, and Tyringham (Bucks)—fifteenth century. Civilian costume ap-peared in brasses from the fourteenth century onwards, as at King's Lynn (Norf)—fourteenth century, Broxbourne (Herts) —fifteenth century, and Staplehurst (Kent)—sixteenth century. Ecclesiastical figures were depicted, as at Higham Ferrers (Northants)—fourteenth century, and so were scholars and professional men, as at Brightwell Baldwin (Oxon).

Two kinds of brasses dating from the fifteenth and sixteenth centuries deserve mention: 'gruesome' brasses showing a skeleton or shrouded figure, as at Margate (Kent); and chrysom brasses representing a child, as at Chesham Bois (Bucks). The figure of the dead person was not always the main feature of the brass. A graceful kind of floriated cross was common, and there is a good example at Taplow (Bucks). Some brasses show scenes from contemporary life, or views, as at Bletchley

(Bucks), while others illustrate religious subjects such as the Life of Christ, as at Sherborne (Hants).

In the thirteenth and early fourteenth centuries, inscriptions were written in Norman French using a Lombardic script. From the later fourteenth until the present century, inscriptions were in Latin or English, and used black letter script—except in the seventeenth and eighteenth centuries, when Roman lettering became fashionable. These remarks apply to stained glass as well. Heraldry played an important part in brass design, and the various devices were sometimes inlaid with enamel colours: otherwise the practice was to fill the lines with black. Early brasses to rich people were often nearly life-size. They were also decorated with canopies—a feature that did not reach its height, however, until the fifteenth century. Brasses gradually became more 'democratic', and consequently might be smaller. All classes were represented, from servants to knights, though with a fairly heavy emphasis on the wealthier middle classes and aristocracy. Most brasses are in the south-east of England, and examples are rare in Scotland and Wales, though there are some examples, as at Betws Cedewain (Powys), and St. Nicholas, Aberdeen.

Tombs and monuments

A great deal of skill and imagination was lavished on tombs and monuments. At first they were simple affairs, consisting in the twelfth and thirteenth centuries of a stone coffin, covered by a slab which was often cut with a cross, and possibly the symbols of the person's rank and occupation—a sword and shield for a knight, a pair of shears, a bell, or a fish for various kinds of tradesmen, and so on. Until the later thirteenth century, covers were narrower at the bottom than at the top. They were often set in the floor so as to be flush with it. Their presence inside the church need not mark the place of burial, which may be in the churchyard. At first only ecclesiastics were buried inside churches, and later on laymen were buried there only if they were wealthy and prominent.

By the thirteenth century, tomb covers were carved with effigies in low relief. From such covers developed table or altar tombs, painted and gilded, and with effigies on top of them. By the fourteenth century, these tombs were often canopied, and set in recesses in the wall, though many were free-standing. Until that time most tombs were made by the master mason, but from then until the sixteenth century his job was taken over by craft centres, especially those concerned in the production of alabaster carvings.

Effigies gradually became less stiff, and by the fifteenth century they could be given more lifelike recumbent poses, though they were still not portraits. By the sixteenth century figures were often shown leaning on one arm, or else kneeling. Some effigies continued to be in the original, reposed attitude, however, with hands together in prayer. In the fifteenth and sixteenth centuries, the sides of tombs were decorated with 'weepers'—small figures of members of the person's family, or of saints and angels. Vaulted and pinnacled canopies reached a pitch of elaboration, and there was a great deal of heraldic decoration. As in brasses, gruesome effigies were sometimes used from the fifteenth to the seventeenth centuries, and there is a fifteenth century example at Feniton (Devon).

After the Reformation, tombs started to include Classical features, and a style developed that prevailed until the late eighteenth century. It involved accurate portraits, and diverting figures and canopies—and if anything, heraldry became even more important. Monuments continued to be Classical in the first part of the nineteenth century, but with the more pensive grace of neo-Classicism.

Though tombs and effigies had occasionally been made of wood, as in the seventeenth century example at Lanreath (Cornwall), from the end of that same century, the standard material was marble. From that time, too, the sculpture became more circumstantial. The textures and styles of wigs and clothes are meticulously observed and, especially in eighteenth century work, symbolic detail abounds, with cherubs and skeletons, urns and hour-glasses. Figures are often shown sitting or standing, poses are languid and theatrical, and drapery becomes more flowing. Waited upon by Truth or Victory or Fame, and dressed as themselves or as Roman heroes, the effigies seem to have woken in some patrician and perfectly appointed heaven.

Though the skill of this sculpture is unfailing, its faults are obvious. It creates form with the obsequiousness of a servant smoothing down his master's coat. But as sculpture it has its moments, and beyond that the men who produced it— John Nost, Scheemakers, Rysbrack and Roubiliac, Nollekens, Westmacott and Flaxman—created from foreign elements an elegiac and essentially English world that still lies hidden in the depths of every shire.

Memorial lettering shared in this general excellence, and

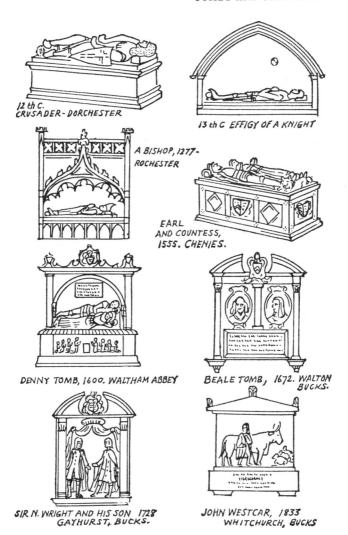

12th C.
CRUSADER - DORCHESTER

13th C EFFIGY OF A KNIGHT

A BISHOP, 1277-
ROCHESTER

EARL
AND COUNTESS,
1555. CHENIES.

DENNY TOMB, 1600. WALTHAM ABBEY

BEALE TOMB, 1672. WALTON
BUCKS.

SIR N. WRIGHT AND HIS SON 1728
GAYHURST, BUCKS.

JOHN WESTCAR, 1833
WHITCHURCH, BUCKS

TOMBS and MEMORIALS

is very well seen in the ledger-stones and wall-tablets of the period, as well as in the larger monuments. Ledger-stones were the equivalents of the earlier tomb-covers, with the difference that carved coats-of-arms and inscriptions were added. Wall-tablets were set in frames, and were sometimes in the scroll-like form of cartouches.

Wall paintings

In the middle ages most churches were adorned with murals painted in the following way. A surface was prepared by covering the wall with plaster, which was allowed to dry and then given a coat of lime-putty. This kind of surface had to be moistened before painting started. An alternative was provided by wet plaster, applied in small areas at a time, and painted directly in the Italian manner of fresco buono—as at Clayton and Coombes (Sussex). The paints were 'distempers' made from lime water, skim milk, and a few simple pigments. These included red and yellow ochre, lime white and lamp black, a green derived from copper salts, and when funds would permit, vermilion and blue.

Most of these medieval wall paintings have disappeared. They were covered over with whitewash at the Reformation, and replaced with texts, as at Abbey Dore (Herefs). Victorian restorers scraped away the plaster because they thought the underlying stone looked better. Many murals have simply deteriorated through lack of renovation. The result is a much depleted body of work, though still one with its own treasures.

Most of the best examples are in the south-east of England, where centres of painting flourished from the twelfth to the fifteenth centuries at such places as Norwich, St. Albans, Westminster, and Canterbury. Many of the painters working at these centres were laymen, not monks as is often supposed. Whichever they were, some of them were outstanding, and several are known by name. Matthew Paris, for example, dominated the St. Albans 'school' in the thirteenth century. Where these painters excelled was in creating lively compositions, and in handling line with faultless, calligraphic ease.

Wall paintings were meant to teach, as well as to be decorative. Like stained glass windows, they set out the characters, traditions, and beliefs of Christianity for those who had no access to religious books. Until the fifteenth century, books were hand-written and rare. Most were in Latin or French, and anyhow the bulk of the population was illiterate.

So saints and their lives were shown, and the Life of the Virgin, as at Croughton (Northants). Saint Christopher's image was frequently painted opposite doorways, since seeing it was supposed to protect the viewer from sudden death. New Testament subjects such as the Nativity and Passion of Christ were common, and Christ's lineage was often summarized in the Tree of Jesse—a kind of pictorial family tree. Some of the most vivid subjects are the moralities warning against blasphemy or the Seven Deadly Sins, for example. These may be contrasted, as at Trotton (Sussex), with the Seven Works of Mercy, such as Feeding the Hungry and Visiting Prisons.

Most spectacular of all, as at St. Thomas, Salisbury (Wilts), was the Doom or Last Judgement of souls, presided over by saints and angels and the figure of Christ. With one hand he makes the sign of the blessing, with the other he judges. This is denoted by the open palm, and in fact a whole range of conventions and gestures was used to make the meaning of a painting clear. The pointing finger signifies condemnation, evil people are shown as physically grotesque, and souls as small, naked figures. Several incidents may be condensed into one scene.

There were also miscellaneous subjects such as the signs of the zodiac, heraldic designs, and purely decorative patterns of diaper work, lined masonry, and scrolls or roses, as at East Wellow (Hants). Twelve consecration crosses were originally painted inside churches, and another twelve were carved on the outside. They were anointed at the consecration of the church. Many examples of both types remain.

There was some fine painting in a more Classical manner after the Reformation, as at Passenham (Northants) and Little Stanmore (London). Figure subjects were generally rarer, however, and more likely to be based on the Old Testament than in former times—both facts that bear witness to Puritan influence. Seventeenth century ceilings were sometimes painted with naive Classical decoration, especially in Scotland, as at Stobhall and St. Mary, Pitcairn (Perths), and Largs (Ayrs), though a similar style can be seen at Bromfield (Salop), for example. Some rich decorative painting was done in Victorian times.

Scotland is not well off when it comes to wall paintings, though there are examples at Turriff (Aberdeens), and Dunkeld (Perths), and there is good Renaissance work at Kinneil, Bo'ness (W. Lothian).

Stained glass windows

The work done in stained glass has hardly been mentioned so far, but it includes some of the craftsman's most illustrious achievements. Old glass has suffered the same neglect and damage as wall paintings, but some magnificent work has survived these vicissitudes. Most of it is in England, though there is a certain amount of old glass in Wales, as at Old Radnor and Presteigne (Powys) and Gresford (Clwyd). Little remains in the churches of Scotland, except for examples such as the fragments in the Magdalene Chapel, Cowgate, Edinburgh.

The purpose and subjects of stained glass were much the same as those of wall paintings, except that the Old Testament was drawn upon more freely, and special subjects were added, such as the Nine Orders of Angels, the Twelve Apostles, and the Twelve Prophets. As with wall paintings, much work emanated from great centres, and in this case they included York, London, Oxford, Canterbury, and other cathedral cities.

Early glass, dating from the twelfth and thirteenth centuries is now rare. The best of it is in the cathedrals of Canterbury and Lincoln, and at York Minster, but there is work in parish churches at Brabourne and Westwell (Kent) and Madley (Herefs), for example. These early windows are in rich blues, reds, and purples, and 'pot-metal' was used—that is, glass coloured right the way through. Later on, by the fifteenth century, glass was sometimes merely 'flashed', or given a coating of coloured glass. Colours were obtained by adding oxides such as those of copper and cobalt to the substances used in making white glass—sand, soda or lime, and potash. The glass was drawn upon, often with great skill, using a dark paint made with copper or iron oxide.

The early period of stained glass produced superlative figure, Jesse, and rose windows and, more commonly, small medallions, which were often enclosed in grisaille glass in the thirteenth century, as at Chartham (Kent) and Stanton Harcourt (Oxon). Grisaille is a clear kind of glass arranged in strapwork, geometrical, or lozenge patterns. It can be cross-hatched or painted with foliage designs, and can also be heightened by touches of colour.

The trends in the fourteenth, fifteenth, and sixteenth centuries can be summed up in the following way. Heraldic windows, which had been introduced towards the end of the thirteenth century, became more popular, and more elaborate.

The same is true of the windows that now came to predomin-ate—figure windows—though they were banned from the time of the Reformation, along with all other religious glass.

Figure windows were surmounted by increasingly ornate canopies. In the fourteenth century, the panels containing each individual design were frequently surrounded with grisaille, and the figures themselves were draped in an S-shaped pose. This had disappeared by the fifteenth century, however, and figure windows were also becoming more complex until, in the form of Subject Windows, they took up all the space available.

By the fifteenth century, too, clear glass was generally in the form of quarries, with subjects such as birds, flowers, and insects drawn upon them. From the fourteenth century on, and especially in the fifteenth century, figures of donors, and possibly of their families as well, were quite often set in quarry glass at the foot of windows. Also from the fourteenth century on, detail—which was sometimes scratched or 'abraded' on flash glass—enveloped figures and filled tracery lights and Jesse windows, as in the fourteenth century examples at Madley (Herefs) and St. Mary, Shrewsbury (Salop). The demand for Jesse windows declined in the fifteenth century, but there are outstanding examples at Mar-garetting (Essex) and Leverington (Cambs).

Settings in the fourteenth century made much use of flat 'architectural' frames, and beautifully stylized foliage and diaper patterns. In the fifteenth century, more attention was paid to the appearance of the everyday world, though a strong decorative element persisted. By the end of the century, poses were more lifelike, and with the invention of perspective, archi-tectural frames were sometimes developed into three-dimen-sional backgrounds for the figures. The tendency towards realism was continued in the sixteenth century, when people were drawn with greater anatomical accuracy, and trappings and architectural detail sometimes included a Classical ele-ment. The fine work at Hillesden (Bucks), for example, shows the results of these changes.

Drawing passed through comparable phases. The strength of the earliest work crystallized in the fourteenth century into rich patterns. This process continued in the fifteenth century, though gradually decorative intensity dispersed and over-lapped with a style that was more naturalistic as well as lighter, and involved stipple and smear as well as line and solid tone. Stained glass drawing throughout the middle ages is distinguished by the skilful use of pure line, one of the main characteristics of English art in all periods—though, again, the manner of this drawing changed from Byzantine convention to a more North European kind of realism.

Colour and texture also became lighter, and greens and yellows were added to the original palette—a wide range of yellows and oranges now being obtainable through the use of silver sulphide or chloride. Though some regret this lightening, it saved stained glass from becoming repetitive, and there is fine fifteenth century work at St Neot (Cornwall), Doddiscombsleigh (Devon), Buckland (Glos), Combs (Suff), and above all at Fairford (Glos).

The invention of a kind of glass 'enamel' paint in the sixteenth century, and the end of continental supplies of pot-metal in the seventeenth, meant that skill in the intricacies of leading and glazing was no longer so necessary—except occasionally in the sphere of heraldry, which gave scope for the virtuosity of such seventeenth century artists as Dininckhoff and Henry Gyles.

Otherwise, two kinds of window became common. Many seventeenth century windows consist of quarries or roundels engagingly painted with emblems, scrolls and mottoes, or natural subjects as before—and sometimes with sundials. But at the same time, a fashion arose for ambitious Italianate picture windows, painted on the glass regardless of the leads, which formed a simple grille. The characteristic work is in the Oxford colleges, but there are also good examples at such places at Lydiard Tregoze (Wilts) and Compton (Surrey). Seventeenth century painters include Van Linge, Richard Greenbury, and Baptista Sutton. Distinguished work was done in the eighteenth century by the Price family, William Peckitt, Francis Eginton, James Pearson, and Thomas Jervais.

Stained glass by this time had become something completely different from medieval work. Though some find it debased and insipid, it makes a pleasant change from earlier styles, and the best of it is fresh and undeniably skilful. But nineteenth century artists were not content with that, and having reintroduced the use of pot-metal, they set about reviving the old methods, styles, and purposes, though the spirit of the age and the force of personality always make themselves felt. Some designers were remarkably successful: Burne-Jones, Rossetti, William Morris, William Eginton, Thomas Willement, C. E. Kempe, Henry Holiday, Nathaniel Westlake, J. P. Seddon, and Pugin all did excellent work, and so did firms such as John Hardman and Co., Clayton and Bell, Betton and Evans, and O'Connor.

There was also a great deal of mediocre work in the nineteenth century—and in the twentieth, which continued the same tradition for a while. Good traditional work was done in this century, however, by Sir Ninian Comper, F. C. Eden, Martin Travers, and Robert Bell, for example—and in a slightly more modern idiom by Evie Hone, Harry Clarke, and J. E. Nutgens. Since then, stained glass has tended to abandon representation, and impact and richness are now often sought in abstract terms and with the help of new materials and techniques. This is sometimes done very effectively, as the work of Ervin Bossanyi, Lawrence Lee, John Piper, and Patrick Reyntiens all shows.

Miscellaneous features

Interior

Churches also contain many utilitarian objects and fittings, but since their interest is historical rather than aesthetic, they will only be mentioned briefly. They include the stools used for supporting coffins during funerals; the shelf or table called a credence, upon which the wafers and wine were placed before their consecration; the Bibles chained to lecterns to prevent theft; and the ringers' rules and records found in the ringing-chambers of towers. Churches sometimes contain libraries of old books, and these may be chained to the shelves.

Then there are the plates, shovels, or ladles made of wood or metal and used in Sunday collections, and the various arrangements made for lighting. Apart from the candelabra already mentioned, these consisted of rushlight holders, taper brackets, candle-sconces, and more rarely of cresset stones—flat stones with a number of wells hollowed in them which were filled with lamp oil. These forms of lighting all caused fumes and smoke, and ventilation was sometimes provided by a side-window set in the south wall of the chancel.

Other features are more unexpected, though the need for them was once plain enough. Ovens were used for baking the wafers for Mass, and cauldrons for brewing the ale needed at church ales or fêtes. The banners and crosses carried in Feast Day processions were kept in tall, narrow banner cupboards. Towers which might be used for defence were sometimes given wooden ladders that could be drawn up into the belfry—instead of the normal fixed ladders, or staircases set in walls or turrets. Extending tongs were sometimes used to control dogs if they disturbed the service. Churches may still keep old pairs of handcuffs, nineteenth century constables' truncheons, fire-buckets, or the fire-hooks used to pull down burning buildings before the flames could spread.

This list is only an indication of the objects to be found in churches, not a full inventory.

The churchyard and its setting

Outside the church, there may be a pillory, whipping-post, ducking-stool, lock-up, or the stocks and, in Scotland, the jougs or the branks. The jougs consisted of an iron collar which was locked round the offender's neck, and fastened to a wall by a chain. The branks, or 'scold's bridle' was used to silence quarrelsome women, for example. Watch houses were built to give shelter for night-watchmen on the look-out for the body-snatchers who dug up corpses in order to sell them to anatomists for dissection. Alternatively, graves might be protected by heavy iron grilles.

There might also be such things as the steps used in mounting horses ridden to church, the eighteenth century stable for the parson's horse, and the village inn formerly used by pilgrims, and often bearing a religious name. Some villages still have the great barns used to store the portion of the tithes that was paid in kind. Tithes were the taxes taken from parishioners for the support of the church and clergy, and theoretically they amounted to one tenth of the annual proceeds of land and labour. There are good examples of tithe barns at Brecon, Great Coxwell (Oxon) (plate 12), Bradford-on-Avon (Wilts), and Whitekirk (E. Lothian).

Many domestic buildings are associated with churches—manor-houses; the church-houses, chapter-houses, rectories, vicarages, and even anchorites' cells inhabited by religious figures; and almshouses, bedehouses, and schoolhouses. Some of these buildings were fortified in early days, and castles or castle-mounds are often found near churches.

Then there may be holy wells; churchyard crosses where sermons were preached; eighteenth century sundials; and the earlier mass dials engraved on the walls of churches, and used to tell the times of services. Masons' marks may be cut in the stone, and so may the symbols and crosses carved by pilgrims. Churchyards may be circular, and this generally denotes pre-Christian origins. There are several examples in central Powys and Dyfed. Lych-gates are quite common, and though most of them are fairly recent, older ones do occur. 'Lych' comes from the Old English word for a corpse, and the lych-gate is the roofed entrance where the coffin was set down before the burial service.

But the main features of a churchyard are the tombs and headstones. Most of these are later than the seventeenth century in date, and some of them have interesting inscriptions. Most burials were on the south side of the church, as the north side was supposed to belong to the Devil: for this reason, the ground is sometimes higher on the south side than elsewhere. The most massive tombs are called table tombs, and they may be surrounded by iron railings. Then come the obelisks and urns, graves set in wall recesses, and the more usual and modest headstones, which in the seventeenth and eighteenth centuries were often works of art, with graceful lettering, shaped heads, and carving in the style of the period.

In the Home Counties, where stone is rare, headstones were sometimes cast in iron, or else the grave was marked with a painted wooden board. The craft of carving stone memorials declined in the nineteenth century, with the introduction of machined uniformity, clumsy lettering, and materials such as white marble and polished granite.

All of these external features contribute towards a unity, which stretches beyond the church itself into the surrounding country or town, and into the past.

6. GLOSSARY

Abacus: the flat slab on top of a capital (q.v.).

Anta: the projection of a side-wall beyond the gable.

Apse: the vaulted semicircular or polygonal end of a chancel or chapel.

Arcade: a row of arches supported on columns.

Ashlar: stone smoothed and squared, and used for facing.

Ballflower: globular flower of three petals enclosing a small ball.

Batter: wall with an inclined face.

Battlements: parapet cut with regular indentions, as in a castle.

Bay: a longitudinal compartment, usually of a building (between, for example, pillars on side walls inside a church, or between windows or buttresses (q.v.) outside).

Beakheads: a motif of heads biting a roll-moulding (q.v.).

Belfry-louvres: the slatted openings in bell-towers.

Billet: ornament of regular raised rectangles.

Blind arcade: an arcade (q.v.) attached to a wall.

Block (or cushion) capital: a capital (q.v.) formed by rounding off the lower angles of a block of stone.

Broken pediment: a pediment (q.v.) with a gap in the base-moulding (see Moulding).

Buttress: a mass of masonry built against, and so supporting a wall.

Camber: slight rise in an otherwise horizontal structure.

Capital: the head of a column.

Chevron: a sculptured zigzag moulding (q.v.).

Choir: the part of the church where the service is sung.

Clerestory: upper storey of nave walls pierced by windows.

Coffering: sunk square or polygonal panels (used to decorate ceilings).

Corbel: block of stone projecting from wall and supporting a weight.

Corbel-table: a series of corbels.

Crow-steps (or corbie-steps): steps in a gable or battlement (q.v.).

Dormer window: window placed vertically in a roof-slope.

Foliated: incorporating carved leaf-shapes.

Groin: the line where two vaults (q.v.) meet.

Keystone: middle stone in an arch.

Lantern: central tower with windows for lighting the crossing below.

Moulding: continuous ornament formed of lines of rolls (see Roll-moulding) and channels.

Ogee: a double curve.

Order: complete column in one of the classical styles. Also— the bands running round a window, doorway, or arch.

Pediment: low-pitched classical 'gable'.

Pier: here, a massive pillar or support.

Portico: centre-piece of building with classical columns and pediment (q.v.).

Roll-moulding: moulding (q.v.) of semicircular or more than semicircular section.

Rustication: smooth-faced, gnarled, or pyramid-faced masonry cut in massive blocks with deep joints.

Sedilia: stone seats for the priests in south wall of chancel.

Splay: chamfer or 'bevel' of a window jamb.

String course: projecting horizontal band or moulding (q.v.) around a building.

Tabernacle-work: elaborate carved canopy-work of the sort found in the tabernacle—the niche or free-standing canopy containing the sacrament.

Transept: the transverse arm of a church.

Transom: horizontal bar across a window.
Triforium: arcaded wall-passage facing the nave, and placed above the arcades (q.v.) and below the clerestory (q.v.).
Tympanum: area between the lintel and arch of a doorway.
Vault: an arched stone ceiling.
Barrel or tunnel vault—of semicircular or pointed section.
Fan vault—one where the ribs open out in a series of elaborate curved fan shapes.
Groined vault—vault formed by two barrel vaults intersecting.
Quadripartite vault—one where one bay (q.v.) of vaulting is divided into four parts.
Rib vault—one with diagonal ribs along groins (q.v.).

---

7. FURTHER READING

Baker, John: *English Stained Glass,* Thames and Hudson.
Betjeman, John: *Collins' Guide to English Parish Churches,* William Collins and Sons.
Caiger-Smith, A.: *English Medieval Mural Paintings,* Oxford, Clarendon Press.
Clarke, Basil and Betjeman, John: *English Churches,* Vista Books.
Cook, M.: *Discovering Brasses and Brass Rubbing,* Shire Publications.
Cox, J. C. and Ford, C.B.: *The Parish Churches of England,* B. T. Batsford Ltd.
Crossley, F. H.: *English Church Craftsmanship,* B. T. Batsford Ltd., 1941.
Fletcher, Sir Banister: *A History of Architecture on the Comparative Method,* Seventeenth edition. Athlone Press, University of London.
Goodhart-Rendel, H. S.: *English Architecture since the Regency,* 1953.
Harries, J.: *Discovering Stained Glass,* Shire Publications.
Hay, George: *The Architecture of Scottish Post-Reformation Churches,* Oxford, Clarendon Press, 1957.
Hutton, G. and Smith, E.: *English Parish Churches,* Thames and Hudson, 1952.
Kersting, A. F., and Vale, E.: *A Portrait of English Churches,* B. T. Batsford Ltd.
Lindsay, I. G.: *The Scottish Parish Kirk,* Saint Andrew Press, Edinburgh.

Pevsner, N.: *The Buildings of England*, Penguin Books.
Rouse, E.C.: *Discovering Wall Paintings*, Shire Publications.
Shell Guides: South-West Wales, Mid Wales, North Wales, Faber and Faber.
Whiffen, M.: *Stuart and Georgian Churches*, B. T. Batsford Ltd., 1947.
Yarwood, Doreen: *The Architecture of England*, B. T. Batsford Ltd.

8. GAZETTEER

Key

Periods
A   Arts and Crafts, or Art Nouveau
C   Classical
Ce   Celtic
G   Gothic (i.e. thirteenth century to seventeenth century) or, in 18G, the Gothick or neo-Gothic of the eighteenth century
N   Norman (Romanesque in Scotland and Ireland), including Transitional
Ro   Roman remains or materials
S   Saxon

Additional information
Col   Collegiate
R   Ruins, or remains
Sec   Secularized
T   Outstanding example of Perpendicular tower
?   Attribution probable but not certain

Architects
RA   Robert Adam
JG   James Gibbs
H   Nicholas Hawksmoor
W   Sir Christopher Wren

Notes
The dating is of significant surviving contributions in order of importance, not in chronological order.

Many churches were restored, rebuilt, or added to in Victorian times. This is not indicated except where the contribution was a radical one.

Unless otherwise stated, eighteenth century work is Classical, and seventeenth, nineteenth, and twentieth century work is Gothic.

ENGLAND

Avon
Banwell (G); Bath Abbey (G); Bristol: All Saints (G, N, 18, 19), St John's (G), Lord Mayor's Chapel (G), St Mary Redcliffe (G); Great Badminton (18); Iron Acton (G, S); Redland (18); Westbury-on-Trym (G); Weston-super-Mare (19, 20); Wrington (GT); Yate (GT); Yatton (GT).

Bedfordshire
Bedford: St Paul (G); Dean (G); Dunstable Priory (N, G); Eaton Bray (G); Elstow (N, G); Felmersham (G); Leighton Buzzard (G); Luton (G); Marston Moretaine (G); Odell (G); Wymington (G).

Berkshire
Avington (N); Lambourn (N, G); Langley Marish (G); Padworth (N, G); Shottesbrooke (G); Wickham (N, 19).

Buckinghamshire
Aylesbury (G); Chetwode (G); Clifton Reynes (G); Edlesborough (G); Gayhurst (18); Hillesden (G); Hitcham (N, G); Little Kimble (G); Little Missenden (G); North Marston (G); Penn (G, 18); Quainton (G); Stewkley (N); Stoke Poges (G); Stowe (G); Tattenhoe (G); Weston Turville (G); Willen (17C); Wing (S); West Wycombe (18, G).

Cambridgeshire
Alconbury (G); Babraham (G); Barnack (S); Bottisham (G); Buckden (G); Burwell (G, N); Cambridge: Holy Sepulchre (N); Castor (N, S); Great Paxton (N, G); Haslingfield (GT); Isleham (G); Landwade (G); Leighton Bromswold (G); Leverington (G); Little Gidding (18); March (G); St Neots (GT); Trumpington (G); Whittlesey (G); Wimpole (18); Wisbech (G); Yaxley (G).

Cheshire
Acton (G, 18G); Astbury (G); Baddiley (G); Bunbury (G); Congleton (18); Great Budworth (G); Lower Peover (G); Malpas (G, 18?, T); Nantwich (G); Over Peover (19, 18, G); Shotwick (G); Wrenbury (G).

Cleveland
Billingham (S, G, 20); Hartlepool (G); Kirkleatham (18, G); Stockton (C).

Cornwall
Altarnun (G); Blisland (G); Chacewater (19); Kilkhampton (G, N); Laneast (G); Lanlivery (GT); Lanteglos-by-Fowey (G); Launcells (G); Launceston (G); Lostwithiel (G); Mullion (G); North Hill (GT); Probus (G); St Austell (GT); St Clement (G); St Endellion (G); St Neot (G).

Cumbria
Armathwaite (G, N); Beckermet (19); Bewcastle (SR); Bolton (N, G); Brougham: St Ninian (G), St Wilfred (G); Cartmel (N, G); Crosthwaite (G); Grasmere (N, G); Isel (N); Kirkby Lonsdale (N, 18); Lanercost (G); Millom (G, N); Ormside (N, G); Over Denton (S, Ro); St Bees (G); Ulpha (G); Wasdale Nether (G); Witherslack (17C).

Derbyshire
Ashbourne (G); Chesterfield (G); Dale Abbey (N); Derby: All Saints (18-JG, G); Eckington (N, G, 18); Melbourne (N); Morley (N, G); Norbury (G); Sandiacre (N, G); Steetley (N); Tideswell (G); Tissington (N); Whitwell (N, G); Wirksworth (G); Youlgreave (N, G).

Devon
Ashcombe (G, 19); Ashton (G); Atherington (G); Branscombe (N, G); Braunton (G, N); Combe Martin (GT); Crediton (G); Cruwys Morchard (G); Cullompton (GT); Exeter: St Mary Arches (N); Harberton (GT); Hartland (G); High Bickington (N, G); Honey-church (N, G); Horwood (G); Ipplepen (GT); Kentisbeare (N); Kenton (G); Molland (G); Ottery St Mary (G); Parracombe (G); Sampford Courtenay (G); Sutcombe (G, N); Swimbridge (G); Tawstock (G); Tiverton: St George (18); Torbryan (G); Widecombe-in-the-Moor (GT).

Dorset
Affpuddle (G, N); Bere Regis (G, N); Blandford (18-J. Bastard, 19); Cerne Abbas (GT); Christchurch (N, G); Colerne (GT); Dorchester (GT); Hilton (G); Kingston (19-G.E. Street); Lyme Regis (G, N); Milton Abbey (G); Puddletown (G); Sher-borne (G, N, S); Studland (N, G); Trent (G); Whitechurch Canonicorum (N, G); Wimborne Minster (N, G); Wimborne St Giles (18, 20); Winterbourne Tomson (N, 18) Worth Mat-ravers (N, G); Yetminster (G).

County Durham
Brancepeth (N, G); Chester-le-Street (G); Escomb (S, Ro); Gibside Chapel (18); Haughton-le-Skerne (G, N); Pittington (N, S?); Seaham (N?, Ro); Sedgefield (G); Staindrop (G, S).

East Sussex
Alfriston (G); Ashburnham (G); Brighton: St Martin, Lewes Road (19), St Peter (19-Sir Charles Barry); Eastbourne: St Mary (G, N); Etchingham (G); Glynde (18); Pevensey (G); Playden (N, G); Rotherfield (G); Rye (G); Winchelsea (GR).

Essex
Bradwell-juxta-Mare (S); Brightlingsea (G); Castle Hedingham (N, G); Copford (N); East Horndon (G); Finchingfield (G, N, 18); Great Bardfield (G); Great Bromley (GT); Great Warley (20A-

H. Townsend); Hatfield Broad Oak (G); Ingatestone (N, G, T); Little Dunmow (G); Little Maplestead (G); Newport (GT); Rivenhall (G); St Osyth (N, G); Saffron Walden (G); Stebbing (G); Thaxted (G); Tilty (G, 18); Wendens Ambo (N).

Gloucestershire

Bibury (G, S, N); Bledington (G, N); Buckland (G); Chedworth (G, N); Cheltenham: St Paul's (19C); Chipping Campden (GT); Cirencester (GT); Daglingworth (S, G); Deerhurst (S); Down Ampney (G); Duntisbourne Rouse (S, N); Elkstone (N, G); Fairford (G); Hailes (G); Kempley (20A); Kempsford (G, N); Newland (G); North Cerney (N, G); Northleach (GT); Oddington (G); Rendcomb (G); Tetbury (18G-Francis Hiorne); Tewkesbury (N, G); Winchcombe (GT).

Greater London

Beddington (G); Camberwell: St George (19C); Camden Town: St Michael (19); Carshalton (G, 18); Chelsea: Holy Trinity, Sloane Street (19A-J. D. Sedding), St Luke, Sydney Street (19-James Savage); City of London: All Hallows, London Wall (18-George Dance, Jnr), St Anne and St Agnes, Aldersgate (17C-W), St Bartholomew-the-Great, Smithfield (N,G), St Benet, Paul's Wharf (17C-W), St Bride, Fleet Street (17C-W); St Dunstan-in-the-West (19-John Shaw), St James Garlickhithe (17C-W), St Katherine Cree (17G+C), St Laurence Jewry (17C-W), St Magnus the Martyr, London Bridge (17C-W), St Margaret Pattens (17C-W), St Martin, Ludgate (17C-W), St Mary Abchurch (17C-W), St Mary Aldermary (17-W), St Mary at-Hill (17C-W), St Mary-le-Bow (17C-W, N), St Mary Somerset (17R-W), St Mary Woolnoth (18-H), St Peter, Cornhill (17C-W), St Stephen, Walbrook (17C-W), St Vedast, Foster Lane (17C-W); Clerkenwell: St James (18); Cranford (G, 18); Croydon: St Michael and All Angels (19-J. L. Pearson); Greenwich: St Alphege (18-H); Harefield (G, 18); Harrow (G, 18); Kensington: Holy Trinity, Kensington Gore (20); Kilburn: St Augustine (19-J. L. Pearson); Limehouse: St Anne (18-H); Northolt (G); Paddington: St Mary Magdalene (19); Petersham: St Peter (G); St Marylebone: All Saints, Margaret Street (19-William Butterfield), All Souls, Langham Place (19C-John Nash), St Cyprian, Clarence Gate (20), St Mary (19-T. Hardwick, Jnr), St Peter, Vere Street (18-JG); St Pancras: New Church (19C, W. & H. W. Inwood); Shoreditch: St Columba, Kingsland Road (19); Spitalfields: Christ Church (18-H); Stepney: St George-in-the-East (18R-H); Stoke Newington: St Matthias (19); Vauxhall: St Peter (19); Wanstead: (18-T. Hardwick); Westminster: St Clement Danes (17C-W, 18-JG), St George, Hanover Square (18-John James), St James, Piccadilly (17C-W), St John, Smith Square (18-Thomas Archer), St Martin-in-the-Fields (18-JG), St Mary-le-Strand (18-JG), St Paul, Covent Garden (17C-Inigo Jones); Whitchurch (18-John James, G).

Greater Manchester
Manchester: St Ann (18), St Thomas, Ardwick Green (18, 19), St Luke, Cheetham (19), St James, Didsbury (G, 18); Salford: Parish Church, Sacred Trinity (18C+G).

Hampshire
Avington (18); Basing (G); Beaulieu (G); Breamore (S); East Meon (N, G); Minstead (G, 18); Pamber Priory Church (N, G); Portchester (N); Romsey (N); Southampton: Church of the Ascension, Bitterne (20); Stoke Charity (G); Winchester: St Cross (N, G), St John (N); Winchfield (N); Wolverton (18); Yateley (S, N, G).

Hereford and Worcester
Abbey Dore (G); Bacton (G); Bishopstone (N, G); Bredon (N); Brinsop (N); Broadway (G); Clodock (G); Croft (G); Croome (18G); Eardisley (G); Eastnor (19, G); Eaton Bishop (G); Elmley Castle (G); Garway (N, G); Great Witley (18); Hereford: All Saints (G); Hoarwithy (19); Holt (N, G); Kilpeck (N, S, G); Leominster (N, G); Little Malvern (G); Madley (G); Malvern (G, N); Martley (N, G); Monnington-on-Wye (G); Much Cowarne (G); Newland (19); Ombersley (19); Pembridge (G); Pershore (G); Richard's Castle (G); St Margaret's (G); Shobdon (18G); Tyberton (18, N); Warndon (N, G); Weobley (GT); Worcester: All Saints (18-Thomas White, G), St Swithin (18).

Hertfordshire
Anstey (N, G); Ashwell (G); Ayot St Lawrence (18-Nicholas Revett); Bishop's Hatfield (G); Bishop's Stortford (G); Hemel Hempstead (N, G); Hitchin (N, G); South Mimms (G); Ware (G); Watford (G).

Humberside
Barton-on-Humber: St Mary (N, G), St Peter (G, S); Beverley: Minster (G), St Mary (GT); Bottesford (G); Bridlington: St Mary (G); Eastrington (N, G); Flamborough (G); Great Coates (GT); Hedon (GT); Holme upon Spalding Moor (GT); Howden (GR); Kingston-upon-Hull: Holy Trinity (GT); Lockington (N, G); Patrington (G); Swine (N, G, 18).

Isle of Wight
Arreton (S, G); Carisbrooke (N, G); Godshill (G); Shorwell (G).

Kent
Ashford (GT); Badlesmere (G); Barfreston (N); Chilham (G); Elham (N, G); Graveney (G, N); Ivychurch (G); Lydd (G, S, T); Mereworth (18); New Romney (N, G); Rainham (G); Ramsgate: St Augustine's R.C. (19-A. W. N. Pugin); Stone (G);

Tenterden (GT); Tunbridge Wells: King Charles the Martyr (17C); Upper Hardres (G); Westwell (G); Wingham (G); Woodchurch (G); Wrotham (G); Wye (G, 18).

Lancashire
Halsall (G); Hoole (G, 18); Lancaster: Priory Church of St Mary's (G); Poulton-le-Fylde (18, G); Rufford (19); Whalley (GT); Woodplumpton (G, 18).

Leicestershire
Bottesford (G); Breedon-on-the-Hill (N, G, S); Church Langton (G); Clipsham (G, N); Empingham (G); Exton (G); Gaddesby (G); Hambleton (N, G); Ketton (N, G); King's Norton (18G); Langham (G); Leicester: St Margaret's (G), St Martin's (G, 19), St Mary de Castro (N, G); Lyddington (G); Melton Mowbray (G); Normanton (18, 19C, 20C); Oakham (G); Peatling Magna (G); Ryhall (G); Stapleford (18G); Staunton Harold (G); Stoke Dry (G, N); Stoke Golding (G); Teigh (18G, G); Thornton (G); Tixover (N, G); Whissendine (G).

Lincolnshire
Boston (GT); Burgh-le-Marsh (G, 18); Caistor (G, N?); Coates-by-Stow (G); Croft (G); Crowland (G, N); Croxby (N, G); Ewerby (G); Folkingham (G, N); Gedney (G); Grantham (G, N); Halton Holegate (GT); Heckington (G); Ingoldmells (G); Irnham (G); Kingerby (N); Langton-by-Partney (18); Leadenham (G); Leake (G); Lincoln: St Benedict (G); Long Sutton (G); Louth (G); Moulton (GT); Saltfleetby (N, G); Sausthorpe (19); Silk Willoughby (G); Skirbeck (G); Spalding (G); Stainfield (18); Stamford: All Saints (G); Stow (N); Tattershall (G); Theddlethorpe All Saints (G); Uffington (G); Westborough (G); Whaplode (N, G); Winthorpe (G); Wrangle (G).

Merseyside
Billinge (18C+G); Liverpool: St James (18), All Hallows, Allerton (19), All Saints, Childwall (G, 19), St Agnes, Sefton Park (19), Holy Trinity, Wavertree (18-John Hope); Sefton (G).

Norfolk
Attleborough (G, N); Beeston-next-Mileham (G); Binham (G); Blakeney (G); Brisley (G); Cawston (G); Cley (G); East Dereham (G); Great Yarmouth (18); Gunton (18-RA); Ingham (G); King's Lynn: St Margaret's (G), St Nicholas (G); Knapton (G); Little Walsingham (G); Ludham (G); North Creake (G); North Runcton (18-Henry Bell); Norwich: St George's-in-Tombland and St John's-on-Timberhill (G), St Peter Mancroft (GT); Ranworth (G); Sall (GT); South Creake (G); Stody (G, N); Swaffham (G); Thorpe Market (18G); Trunch (G); Walpole

St Peter (G); Warham (G); West Walton (G); Wiggenhall St German (G); Wiggenhall St Mary Magdalene (G); Wiveton (G); Worstead (G); Wymondham (G, N, T).

Northamptonshire
Aldwincle (GT); Aynho (18, G); Brixworth (S, Ro, N, G); Daventry (18-David Hiorn); Earls Barton (S, N); Fothering-hay (G); Higham Ferrers (G); Kettering (G); Kings Sutton (G, 19); Lowick (GT); Northampton: All Saints (17-Henry Bell?, G), Holy Sepulchre (N, G), St Peter (N, G); Oundle: St Peter (G); Titchmarsh (GT); Warmington (G); Wellingborough: St Mary (20-Sir Ninian Comper); Whiston (GT).

Northumberland
Alnwick (G); Blanchland (G); Bolam (N, S); Hexham (G, S, Ro, 20); Kirknewton (G); Kirkwhelpington (N, G, 18); Morpeth: St Mary the Virgin (G); Ovingham (G, S); Ponteland (N, G); Seaton Delaval (N).

North Yorkshire
Alne (G, N, C); Bedale (G); Bolton Percy (G); Bossall (N, G); Coxwold (G); Easby (G); Hemingbrough (G); Old Malton (G, N); Scarborough: St Mary (G); Selby Abbey (N, G); Skelton (19-William Burges); Studley Royal (19-William Burges); Thirsk (G); Wensley (G); Whitby: St Mary (N); Wintringham (G, N); York: All Saints, North Street (G), All Saints, Pavement (G), St Denys (N, G), Holy Trinity, Goodramgate (G, 18), Holy Trinity, Micklegate (G, N, 19), St Martin-cum-Gregory (G, 18, Ro), St Mary, Castlegate (N, G), St Michael-le-Belfry (G), St Olave (G, 18C+G).

Nottinghamshire
Blyth (N); East Markham (G); Egmanton (N); Hawton (G); Newark (G); Nottingham: St Mary (G); Teversal (N, G).

Oxfordshire
Abingdon (G); Adderbury (G); Bloxham (G); Burford (G); Compton Beauchamp (G); Dorchester (G); Ewelme (G); Iffley (N, G); North Moreton (G); Nuneham Courtenay (18-James Stuart); Oxford: All Saints (18), St Mary the Virgin (G, 17C-Nicholas Stone); Rycote (G); Sparsholt (G); Stanton Harcourt (G); Sutton Courtenay (G); Thame (N, G); Uffington (G); Yarnton (G).

Salop
Kinlet (G, N); Langley Chapel (G); Ludlow (G); Lydbury North (N, G); Melverley (G); Onibury (N); Richard's Castle (19); St Martin's (G); Shrewsbury: St Chad (18-George Steuart), St Mary (N, G); Tong (G); Whitchurch (18).

Somerset
Batcombe (G, 18, T); Bishop's Lydeard (GT); Bruton (G, 18); Chewton Mendip (N, G, T); Crewkerne (G); Croscombe (G); Dunster (G, N); East Brent (G); Glastonbury: St John the Baptist (GT); High Ham (G); Huish Episcopi (G, N. T); Ilminster (GT); Isle Abbots (GT); Kingsbury Episcopi (GT); Martock (G); Mells (G); North Cadbury (G); North Curry (G, N); North Petherton (GT); Selworthy (G); Stogursey (N, G); Stoke-sub-Hamdon (N, G); Swell (G, N); Taunton (G. 19, T); Trull (G); Wedmore (G, N); Wells (GT); Weston Zoyland (GT); West Pennard (G).

South Yorkshire
Ecclesfield (G); Fishlake (N, G); Rotherham (G); Sheffield: St Peter (G, 18); Tickhill (GT).

Staffordshire
Alrewas (G); Blymhill (G); Checkley (N, G); Clifton Campville (G); Eccleshall (G); Hamstall Ridware (G); Hoar Cross (19); Ingestre (17C-W); Mayfield (N, G); Norbury (G, 18G); Penkridge (G); Rushton (G, 19); Stafford: Collegiate Church of St Mary (G, 19, S); Tamworth (N, G); Tutbury (N, 19).

Suffolk
Aldenburgh (G); Beccles (GT); Blythburgh (G); Bury St Edmunds: St Mary (G); Clare (G); Combs (G); Dalham (G); Dennington (G); Denston (G); Euston (17C); Eye (GT); Framlingham (GT); Fressingfield (G); Gislingham (G); Kedington (G); Lavenham (GT); Long Melford (G, 20); Mildenhall (G); Needham Market (G); Southwold (G); Stoke-by-Nayland (GT); Sudbury: St Gregory (G); Ufford (G); Wenhaston (G); Wingfield (G); Wissington (N); Woodbridge (G); Woolpit (G).

Surrey
Betchworth (G, N); Chipstead (G); Compton (N); Esher (G, 18); Gatton (19); Great Bookham (N, G); Guildford: St Mary (N, S, G); Holmbury St Mary (19); Mickleham (N, G); Ockham (G); Shere (G); Stoke d'Abernon (S, G); Wotton (G, N).

Tyne and Wear
Jarrow (S); Monkwearmouth (S); Newcastle: All Saints (18), St Andrew (G, 18), St Ann (18), St Nicholas (G); Roker (20A -E. S. Prior); Tynemouth: Christ Church (18).

Warwickshire
Astley (G); Brailes (G); Coleshill (G); Compton Wynyates (G); Preston-on-Stour (18G); Stratford-upon-Avon (G, 18); Warwick: St Mary (17-Sir William Wilson, G); Wootton Wawen (S).

West Midlands
Berkswell (N); Binley (18-RA?); Birmingham: St Agatha,
Sparkbrook (19), St Peter and St Paul, Aston (G, 19), St Philip
(18-Thomas Archer); Castle Bromwich (18, G); Wolver-
hampton: Collegiate Church of St Peter (G), St John (18-
William Baker).

West Sussex
Amberley (NG); Bosham (S, G); Boxgrove (N, G); Burton
(N); Findon (G); Hardham (N); Lowfield Heath (19); New
Shoreham (N, G); Old Shoreham (N); Sompting (S, N);
South Harting (G); Steyning (N, G); Trotton (G); West
Chiltington (N, G); West Grinstead (G); Worth (S).

West Yorkshire
Adel (N); Almondbury (G); Halifax: St John the Baptist (G);
Horbury (18-John Carr); Leeds: Holy Trinity (18), St Bar-
tholomew, Armley (19), St John Briggate (G), St Michael,
Headingley (19); Wakefield (G).

Wiltshire
Bishops Cannings (G, N); Bishopstone (S. Wilts) (G); Bradford
-on-Avon: Holy Trinity (N, G), St Laurence (S); Cricklade (N,
G, T); Edington (G); Farley (17C-W?); Great Chalfield (G);
Hardenhuish (18-John Wood, Junior); Heytesbury (N, G);
Lacock (G); Lydiard Tregoze (G); Malmesbury (G, N); Mere
(G, N, T); Mildenhall (G, N); Potterne (G); Purton (G);
Salisbury: St Thomas of Canterbury (G); Steeple Ashton (G);
Stratford Tony (G); Tisbury (G, N, 18); Wanborough (GT);
Westwood (G, 18); Wilton (19-T. H. Wyatt and David Bran-
don); Winterbourne Bassett (G).

WALES
Clwyd
Bangor Is-coed (18); Bodelwyddan (19); Caerwys (G, 18);
Cefn Meiriadog (19); Chirk (N, G); Cilcain (G); Denbigh:
Whitchurch (G); Diserth (G); Efenechdyd (G); Gresford
(GT); Holt (G); Holywell: St Winifred's Chapel (G); Hope
(G); Llanarmon-yn-Ial (18C+G, 19); Llanelidan (G); Llan-
gollen (G, 18, 19); Llangynhafel (G); Llannefydd (G); Llan-
rhaeadr-yn-Cinmerch (G); Llansilin (G, 19); Llanynys (G, 18G
+C); Mold (G, 18G, T); Northop (GT); Overton (G); Ruthin
(G, 19); St Asaph (G); Treuddyn (19); Whitford (G); Worth-
enbury (18); Wrexham (GT).

Dyfed
Abergwili: Llanfihangel Uwch Gwili (G, 19); Beddgelert (G);
Bletherston (N, 19); Cardigan (G); Carew (G); Carmarthen
(G); Castlemartin (G); Cilycwm (G); Goodwick (20); Gum-
freston (G); Haverfordwest: St Martin (N, G), St Mary (G);
Hodgeston (G); Kidwelly (G); Laugharne (G); Llanarth (G);

Llanbadarn Fawr (N); Llandawke (G); Llanddewi (G, Ce);
Llandeilo (G, 19); Llandovery (G); Llandyssul (G, N, Ce);
Llanfihangel-ar-Arth (G); Llanfihangel-y-Creuddyn (G); Llan-
fynydd (G); Llangoedmore (18); Llanilar (G); Llanrhystyd
(G); Llansantffraid (G); Llanstephan (G); Llanwnen (G);
Manorbier (N, G); Manordeifi (G); Monkton (G); Mwnt (G);
Myddfai (G); Narberth (G); Nevern (G); Newport (G);
Pembrey (G); Pembroke: St Mary (G); Prendergast (N, 19);
Rhoscrowther (N, G); Robeston West (N, G); Rudbaxton (N,
G); St Clears (N); St Florence (N, G); St Ishmaels (G);
Stackpole (N, G); Talley (18); Tenby (G); Tremain (G).

Gwent
Abergavenny (G, 19); Bettws-Newydd (G); Caerleon (N, G);
Caerwent (G, Ro); Chepstow (N); Dixton (N); Grosmont (N,
G); Llanelli (N, G); Llangoven (N, G); Llangwm Uchaf (G);
Llantilio Crossenny (G); Llantilio Pertholey (G); Magor (N,
G); Mathern (G); Monmouth: St Mary (G, 19); Newport:
St Woolos (N, G); Peterstone (G); Raglan (G); Redwick (G);
St Brides Wentlooge (G); Skenfrith (G); Trelleck (G); Usk
(N, G).

Gwynedd
Aberdaron (N, G); Aberffraw: St Beuno (N, G); Amlwch (18);
Beaumaris (G); Beddgelert (N, G, 19); Betws-y-coed (G);
Clynnog Fawr (G); Conway (N, G); Corwen (G, Ce); Dol-
gellau (18); Dolwyddelan (G); Holyhead: St Cybi (G, 19);
Llanaber (N); Llanaelhaearn (N); Lanbabo (N, G); Llan-
bedrog (G); Llandderfel (G); Llanddwywe-is-y-Graig (G);
Llandrillo (G); Llandwrog (19); Llandyfrydog (G); Llanegryn
(G); Llaneilian (N, G); Llanengan (G); Llanfaglan (G);
Llanfair (G); Llangadwaladr (N, G, 19); Llangeinwen (N, 19);
Llangelynin (G); Llangristiolus (G); Llangwyllog (G); Llan-
gwynnadl (G); Llaniestyn (G); Penmon (N); Trefriw: Llan-
rhychwyn Church (G); Tywyn (N).

Mid Glamorgan
Coity (G); Coychurch (G); Ewenny Priory (N, G, 19); New-
ton Nottage (G).

Powys
Aberedw (G); Alltmawr (G); Bettws Cedewain (G); Bettws
Disserth (19); Bleddfa (G); Brecon: St Mary (N, G); Bryn-
gwyn (G); Cascob (G); Colva (G); Cregrina (G); Crickadarn
(G); Crickhowell (G); Crigglon (18, 19); Cwmbach-llechryd
(19-J. B. Fowler); Devynock (G); Disserth (G); Glascwm (G);
Kerry (N); Llananno (G); Llanbister (G); Llanbrynmair (G);
Llanddew (G); Llandefalle (G); Llandeilo Graban (G); Llan-
elieu (N, G); Lanfihangel-Cwmdu (N, G); Llanfilo (N, G);
Llanfyllin (18); Llangammarch Wells (20); Llangasty-
Talyllyn (19-J. L. Pearson); Llangattock (N, G); Llangenny
(G); Llanidloes (G); Llanllugan (G); Llanllwchaiarn (19C);
Llanwnog (G); Llanwrin (G); Llan-y-wern (G); Meifod (N);

Merthyr-Cynog (N); Montgomery (G); Old Radnor (G); Partrishow (G); Pennant Melangell (N, 18); Presteigne (N, G); Rhulen (G); Tregynon (G); Ystradfellte (G).

South Glamorgan
Cardiff: St John (GT); Colwinston (G); Gileston (G); Llansannor (N); Llantwit Major (G); Marcross (N); St Hilary (N).

West Glamorgan
Cheriton (G); Ilston (G); Llangennith (N); Llangyfelach (G); Llanmadog (G); Margam (N, G, 19); Rhosili (N).

SCOTLAND

Aberdeenshire
Aberdeen: King's College Chapel (G); North Church (19C-John Smith); St. Nicholas (18-JG, 19, G); Auchindoir (19, GR); Bourtie (19C+G); Echt (19); Fraserburgh; Old (19C); Gartly (G); Glenbuchat (G, 18); Kildrummy (19, G); Kincardine O'Neil (GR); Kinkell (G); Kintore (G); Monymusk (NR); Peterhead; Old (19C, G, N); Pitsligo (G, 19); Tarves (18); Towie (G); Turriff (18, G, 19).

Angus
Arbroath; Inverbrothock (19C); Brechin (now Cathedral) (G, Ce, 19); Careston (G); Cawdor (G); Craig (18G, 19); Dundee: St. Andrew's (18-Samuel Bell); St. Mary's (GT); Farnell (19); Forfar; Lowson Memorial (20); Glamis (18, G); Inverarity (18, 19); Kirriemuir (20); Logie Pert (19, 18, GR); Montrose: Old (18, 19); St. John's (19C).

Argyll
Dunstaffnage Chapel (G); Eileach-an-Naoimh Chapel, Garvellach Islands (Ce); Glenorchy (19); Inveraray (18-Robert Mylne); Iona: St. Oran's Chapel (NR); Parliamentary Kirk (19-Thomas Telford); Kilarrow, Isle of Islay (19); Skipness; St. Brendan's Chapel (G).

Ayrshire
Ayr; Auld Kirk (G, 20); Dailly (18); Dreghorn (18); Fenwick (G, 19); Irvine; Relief (18); Kilbirnie (G, 18); Kilmarnock: Laigh (19, G); Old High (18, 19); Kilmaurs (G, 19); Kirkmichael (18); Kirkoswald (18); Largs (G); Symington (N); Tarbolton (19C).

Banffshire
Banff; St. Mary's (18, 19, G); Boyndie (18); Cullen (G, Col); Deskford (G); Grange (18); Mortlach (G).

Berwickshire
Bunkle (NR); Channelkirk (19); Chirnside (N); Coldstream (19C); Eccles (18); Fogo (18, G); Greenlaw (G, 18, 19); Lauder; Old (17-Sir William Bruce); Legerwood (NR); Polwarth (18).

Bute
St. Blane's (G).

Caithness
Canisbay (G, 18); Crosskirk; St. Mary's (N); Dunnet (G, 19); Reay (18); Thurso (GR, N).

Clackmannanshire
Alloa; St. Mungo's (19, G); Clackmannan (19).

Dumfriesshire
Dumfries; St. Michael's (18); Durisdeer (G); Ruthwell (19, Ce).

Dunbartonshire
Cumbernauld; St. Ninian's (G); Kilmaronock (19C).

East Lothian
Dirleton (17C+G); Dunglass (GR); Gullane (N); Haddington (GR); Pencaitland (G); Prestonkirk; Old (18, G, 19); Saltoun (19); Seton (G, Col); Spott (18, G); Tyningham (NR); Whitekirk (G); Yester (18, G).

Fife
Abdie (19, GR); Aberdour (G, N); Anstruther Easter (G); Anstruther Wester (18, G); Burntisland; St. Columba's (G, 18); Ceres (19C+G); Collessie (19); Crail (G, Col); Cupar; Old (18, 19, G); Dairsie (G); Elie (18, G, 19); Kilmany (18); Leuchars (N, G); Markinch; St. Drostan's (18, N, 19); Monimail (18, 19, G); Newburn (19); Pittenweem (19, G); St. Andrews: Holy Trinity (G, 20); St. Regulus' Church (NR); University Chapels of St. Salvator and St. Leonard (G); St. Monan's (G).

Inverness-shire
Harris; Rowdil (G); Inverness; Old High (18, G); Kirkhill (18, G).

Kincardineshire
Arbuthnott (G); Benholme (19C); Cowie (GR).

Kinross-shire
Portmoak (19).

Kirkcudbrightshire
Buitle (GR); Lincluden (GR, Col); Terregles (G, 19).

Lanarkshire
Biggar (G, Col); Bothwell (G, N, 19); Carnwath (GR); Carstairs (18); Douglas (NR); Glasgow: Barony (19); Barony North Church (19C); Belhaven-Westbourne Church (19C); Caledonia Road Free Church (19C-Alexander Thomson); Camphill, Queen's Park Church (19); Elgin Place Church (19C); Grey-

friars (19C); Kelvingrove Parish Church (19C); Lansdowne Church (19); Park Church (19); Queen's Cross (19A-C. R. Mackintosh); St. Andrew's (18-Allan Dreghorn); St. Bride's Episcopal (20); St. George's-in-the-Fields (19C); St. George's Tron Church (19C); St. Margaret's, Knightswood Road (20); St. Vincent Street (19C); Tron (Sec 18GT); Hamilton; Old (18-William Adam); Lanark; Old (18); Libberton (19); Pettinain (G).

Midlothian

Borthwick (N, G); Carrington (18); Crichton (G); Currie (18, G); Dalkeith (GR); Edinburgh: Canongate (17C-James Smith); Corstorphine (G); Duddingstone (G, N, 19); Greyfriars (G, 18); Magdalene Chapel, Cowgate (G); North Leith (19C); St. Andrew's (18-Andrew Frazer and William Sibbald); St. Cuthbert's (19C, 18); St. George's (19C-Robert Reid); St. Giles (now Cathedral) (G); St. John's Episcopal (19); St. Margaret's Chapel, Edinburgh Castle (N, G); St. Mary's (19C-Thomas Brown); St. Stephen's (19C-W. H. Playfair); Tolbooth Church (19); Tron (17G + C-John Mylne, 19); Mid Calder (G, 19); Musselburgh; Inveresk (19); Newbattle (18); Penicuik; St. Mungo's (18); Ratho (N); Roslin (G, Col).

Moray

Birnie (N); Dyke (18); Elgin; St. Giles's (19C-Archibald Simpson); Fochabers; Bellie (18); Spynie (18).

Nairnshire

Auldearn (18, GR); Cawdor (G, 19).

Orkney

Birsay; St. Peter's (NR); Egilsay (NR); Orphir; St. Nicholas (NR); Wyre; St. Mary's Chapel (NR).

Peebleshire

Lyne (G); Stobo (N, G).

Perthshire

Abernethy; Round tower (N); Comrie; Old (19); Dunning (N); Foulis Easter (G); Innerpeffray (G); Kenmore (18G, GR); Kincardine-in-Menteith (19, 20); Kinfauns (GR); Methven (18, 19, G); Muthill (N, G); Perth: St. John's (G); St. Leonard's (19C-William Mackenzie); Stobhall (G); Tullibardine (G, Col).

Renfrewshire

Eaglesham (18); Greenock: Mid Kirk (18); West (19); Inchinnan (20); Inverkip (19C); Johnstone; High (18G); Lochwinnoch; St. John's (19); Mearns (18, 19); Neilston; Old (18); Paisley: High (18); St. George's (19C).

Ross and Cromarty

Cromarty (18); Dingwall (19C + G); Kilchrist (G).

Roxburghshire
Bowden (G, 20); Cavers (G, Sec); Eckford (G, 18); Kelso; Old (18); Linton (G); Roxburgh (18, 19).

Selkirkshire
Ettrick (19); Yarrow (G).

Shetland
Tingwall (18).

Stirlingshire
Kippen (G); Stirling: Chapel Royal of Stirling Castle (G+C); Holy Rood (G).

Sutherland
Farr (18); Golspie (18, G); Rogart (18).

West Lothian
Abercorn (N, 18); Dalmeny (N); Kirkliston (N, G); Linlithgow (G); South Queensferry (G); Torphichen (18); Uphall (N, G, 19).

Wigtownshire
Cruggleton (N); Glasserton (18, 19, G); Port William; Chapel Finian (N); Isle of Whithorn; Chapel (Ce, G, N).

NORTHERN IRELAND

Antrim
Antrim: Parish Church (G, 19); Round tower, Steeple House grounds (Ce); Armoy; Protestant Church (G); Ballinderry; Middle Church (G); Ballycastle (18); Belfast: Christ Church, College Square North (19C-William Farrell); Cooke Memorial Church, May Street (19C-W. Smith); First Presbyterian (now Unitarian) Church, Rosemary Street (18-Roger Mulholland); St. George's, High Street (18, 19C-John Bowden); St. Mark, Dundela (19-William Butterfield); St. Matthew's, Woodvale Road (19); Carrickfergus; St. Nicholas (G, N, 18); Dunmurry; Presbyterian Church (18); Gracehill (18); Lisburn (now Cathedral of St. Saviour) (G, 19); Randalstown, Presbyterian Church (18G+C).

Armagh
Killevy: West Church (Ce); East Church (G); Kilmore (G, Ce); Lurgan (G, 19).

Down
Bangor: Abbey Church (G, 18, 20); First Presbyterian Church (G); Castlereagh, Presbyterian Church (19C); Donaghadee (G, N, 19); Downpatrick (G, N, 18); Drumbeg (18G); Hillsborough (18G, G); Hilltown (18G); Holywood; Unitarian Church (19C); Killyleagh (G); Loughbrickland; Presbyterian Church (G); Moira (18, 19);

Newry: St. Mary (19); St. Patrick's (G); Unitarian Church (19C); Newtonbreda (18, 19); Rademon; Presbyterian Church (18); Saintfield (18G, 19); St. John's Point, near Killough (Ce R); Waringstown (G, 18, 19).

Fermanagh

Aghalurcher (18); Boho (G); Devenish, Lower Lough Erne: Round tower (N); St. Molaise's House (NR); Great Church (R); St. Mary's Priory (GR); Enniskillen (now Cathedral of St. Macartan (G, 19); Monea; Protestant Church (G); White Island, Lower Lough Erne (Ce R).

Loudonderry

Banagher: Magheramore Abbey (N); Tomb (Ce?R); Bovevagh, near Dungiven: Church (GR); Tomb (Ce?R); Coleraine (G, 19); Culmore (G); Dungiven Priory (NR, GR); Maghera (NR).

Tyrone

Ballynaclog (G); Benburb (G, 19); Castlecaulfeild, near Dungannon (G, 19); Clonoe, Killary Glebe (G); Dungannon (18, 19); Omagh (19); Urney, near Strabane; Presbyterian Church (G).

ISLE OF MAN

Douglas; St. Matthew (19); Kirk Braddan; Old Church (18); Kirk Malew (18).

PHOTOGRAPHS

Photographs are acknowledged as follows: Robert D. Bristow, plates 13, 15; Grantham Journal Co Ltd, plate 6; Emrys Jones, plate 9; Cadbury Lamb, plates 1, 2, 3, 4, 5, 7, 10, 11, 12, 14, 16, 17, 18; John A. Long, plate 8; D. Uttley, plate 18.